Teacher's Handbook

Karen Hamilton

OXFORD
UNIVERSITY PRESS

OXFORD
UNIVERSITY PRESS

198 Madison Avenue
New York, NY 10016 USA

Great Clarendon Street, Oxford OX2 6DP UK

Oxford University Press is a department of the University of Oxford.
It furthers the University's objective of excellence in research, scholarship, and education by publishing worldwide in

Oxford New York

Auckland Cape Town Dar es Salaam Hong Kong Karachi
Kuala Lumpur Madrid Melbourne Mexico City Nairobi
New Delhi Shanghai Taipei Toronto

With offices in

Argentina Austria Brazil Chile Czech Republic France Greece
Guatemala Hungary Italy Japan Poland Portugal Singapore
South Korea Switzerland Thailand Turkey Ukraine Vietnam

General Manager, American ELT: Laura Pearson
Publisher: Stephanie Karras
Associate Publishing Manager: Sharon Sargent
Development Editor: Kelley Perrella
Associate Development Editor: Keyana Shaw
Director, ADP: Susan Sanguily
Executive Design Manager: Maj-Britt Hagsted
Associate Design Manager: Michael Steinhofer
Electronic Production Manager: Julie Armstrong
Production Artist: Elissa Santos
Cover Design: Michael Steinhofer
Production Coordinator: Elizabeth Matsumoto

ISBN: 978-0-19-475630-3 Reading and Writing 4 Teacher's Handbook Pack
ISBN: 978-0-19-475655-6 Reading and Writing 4 Teacher's Handbook
ISBN: 978-0-19-475665-5 Reading and Writing/ Listening and Speaking 4 Testing Program CD-ROM
ISBN: 978-0-19-475643-3 Q Online Practice Teacher Access Code Card

Printed in China

This book is printed on paper from certified and well-managed sources

10 9 8 7 6 5 4 3 2 1

ACKNOWLEDGMENTS

The publishers would like to thank the following for their kind permission to reproduce photographs:
p. vi Marcin Krygier/iStockphoto; xiii Rüstem GÜRLER/iStockphoto

CONTENTS

WELCOME TO Q: Skills for Success

Q: Skills for Success is a six-level series with two strands, *Reading and Writing* and *Listening and Speaking.*

STUDENT AND TEACHER INFORMED

Q: Skills for Success is the result of an extensive development process involving thousands of teachers and hundreds of students around the world. Their views and opinions helped shape the content of the series. *Q* is grounded in teaching theory as well as real-world classroom practice, making it the most learner-centered series available.

To the Teacher

Highlights of the *Q: Skills for Success* Teacher's Handbook

LEARNING OUTCOMES

As you probably know from your own teaching experience, students want to know the point of a lesson. They want to know the "why" even when they understand the "how." In the classroom, the "why" is the learning outcome, and to be successful, students need to know it. The learning outcome provides a clear reason for classroom work and helps students meaningfully access new material.

Each unit in Oxford's *Q: Skills for Success* series builds around a thought-provoking question related to that unit's unique learning outcome. Students learn vocabulary to answer the unit question; consider new information related to the unit's theme that utilizes this vocabulary; use this information to think critically about new questions; and use those answers to practice the new reading, vocabulary, grammar, and writing skills they need to achieve the unit's learning outcome.

Each aspect of the learning process in the Q series builds toward completing the learning outcome. This interconnected process of considering new information is at the heart of a critical thinking approach and forms the basis of the students' work in each unit of the Q series. At the end of the unit, students complete a practical project built around the learning outcome.

Learning outcomes create expectations in the classroom: expectations of what students will learn, what teachers will teach, and what lessons will focus on. Students benefit because they know they need to learn content for a purpose; teachers benefit because they can plan activities that reinforce the knowledge and skills students need to complete the learning outcome. In short, learning outcomes provide the focus that lessons need.

UNIT 6 *Unit* QUESTION
What makes you laugh?

Laughter

READING • identifying the topic sentence in a paragraph
VOCABULARY • using the dictionary
GRAMMAR • sentences with *when*
WRITING • writing a topic sentence

LEARNING OUTCOME
Explain what makes you or someone you know laugh.

In this example unit, students are asked to think about and discuss what makes them laugh.

The unit assignment ties into that unit's unique learning outcome.

Writing a Paragraph	20 points	15 points	10 points	0 points
The first line of the paragraph is indented, and the paragraph has an appropriate topic sentence.				
Sentences with *when* and *because* are correct.				
Paragraph explains what makes someone laugh using vocabulary from the unit.				
Sentences begin with capital letters and end with appropriate punctuation.				
Every sentence has a subject and a verb and they are in agreement.				

Total points: _______________

Comments:

Clear assessments allow both teachers and students to comment on and measure learner outcomes.

▶ *Reading and Writing 1, page 116*

Unit Assignment: Write a paragraph about what makes someone laugh

Unit Question (5 minutes)

Refer students back to the ideas they discussed at the beginning of the unit about laughter. Ask: *What makes you or someone you know laugh?* Bring out the answers students wrote on poster paper at the beginning of the unit. Cue students if necessary by asking specific questions about the content of the unit: *Why is laughter important? What makes you laugh the hardest? What kinds of things do you find funny? What kinds of things are not funny?* Read the direction lines for the assignment together to ensure understanding.

Learning Outcome

1. Tie the Unit Assignment to the unit learning outcome. Say: *The outcome for this unit is to explain what makes you or someone you know laugh. This Unit Assignment is going to let you show your skill at writing paragraphs, using a topic sentence, and writing sentences with* when *and* because.

CRITICAL THINKING

A critical thinking approach asks students to process new information and to learn how to apply that information to a new situation. Teachers might set learning outcomes to give students targets to hit—for example: "After this lesson, give three reasons why people immigrate"—and the materials and exercises in the lesson provide students with the knowledge and skills to think critically and discover *their* three reasons.

Questions are important catalysts in the critical thinking process. Questions encourage students to reflect on and apply their knowledge to new situations. Students and teachers work together to understand, analyze, synthesize, and evaluate the lesson's questions and content to reach the stated outcomes. As students become more familiar with these stages of the critical thinking process, they will be able to use new information to complete tasks more efficiently and in unique and meaningful ways.

Tip Critical Thinking

In Activity B, you have to **restate**, or say again in perhaps a different way, some of the information you learned in the two readings. **Restating** is a good way to review information.

Throughout the Student Book, *Critical Thinking Tips* accompany certain activities, helping students to practice and understand these critical thinking skills.

B (10 minutes)

1. Introduce the Unit Question, *Why do people immigrate to other countries?* Ask related information questions or questions about personal experience to help students prepare for answering the more abstract unit question: *Did you immigrate to this country? What were your reasons for leaving your home country? What were your reasons for choosing your new country? What did you bring with you?*
2. Tell students: *Let's start off our discussion by listing reasons why people might immigrate. For example, we could start our list with* finding work *because many people look for jobs in new countries. But there are many other reasons why people immigrate. What else can we think of?*

Critical Thinking Tip (1 minute)

1. Read the tip aloud.
2. Tell students that restating also helps to ensure that they have understood something correctly. After reading a new piece of information, they should try to restate it to a classmate who has also read the information, to ensure that they both have the same understanding of information.

The *Q Teacher's Handbook* features notes offering questions for expanded thought and discussion.

CRITICAL Q EXPANSION ACTIVITIES

The *Q Teacher's Handbook* expands on the critical thinking approach with the Critical Q Expansion Activities. These activities allow teachers to facilitate more practice for their students. The Critical Q Expansion Activities supplement the *Q Student Book* by expanding on skills and language students are practicing.

In today's classrooms, it's necessary that students have the ability to apply the skills they have learned to new situations with materials they have never seen before. Q's focus on critical thinking and the *Q Teacher's Handbook's* emphasis on practicing critical thinking skills through the Critical Q Expansion Activities prepares students to excel in this important skill.

Critical Q: Expansion Activity

Outlining

1. Explain to students: *A popular way to prepare to outline one's ideas is to use a cluster map. In a cluster map, a big circle is drawn in the middle of a page or on the board, and a main point is written inside it—**this will become the topic sentence in the outline.***
2. Then explain: *Next, lines are drawn away from the circle and new, smaller circles are attached to the other end of those lines. Inside each of the smaller circles, ideas are written which relate to the main point—**these become supporting sentences in the outline.***

The easy-to-use activity suggestions increase student practice and success with critical thinking skills.

21ST CENTURY SKILLS

Both the academic and professional worlds are becoming increasingly interdependent. The toughest problems are solved only when looked at from multiple perspectives. Success in the 21st century requires more than just core academic knowledge—though that is still crucial. Now, successful students have to collaborate, innovate, adapt, be self-directed, be flexible, be creative, be tech-literate, practice teamwork, and be accountable—both individually and in groups.

Q approaches language learning in light of these important 21st Century Skills. Each unit asks students to practice many of these attributes, from collaboration to innovation to accountability, *while* they are learning new language and content. The *Q Student Books* focus on these increasingly important skills with unique team, pair, and individual activities. Additionally, the *Q Teacher's Handbooks* provide support with easy-to-use 21st Century Skill sections for teachers who want to incorporate skills like "openness to other people's ideas and opinions" into their classrooms but aren't sure where to start.

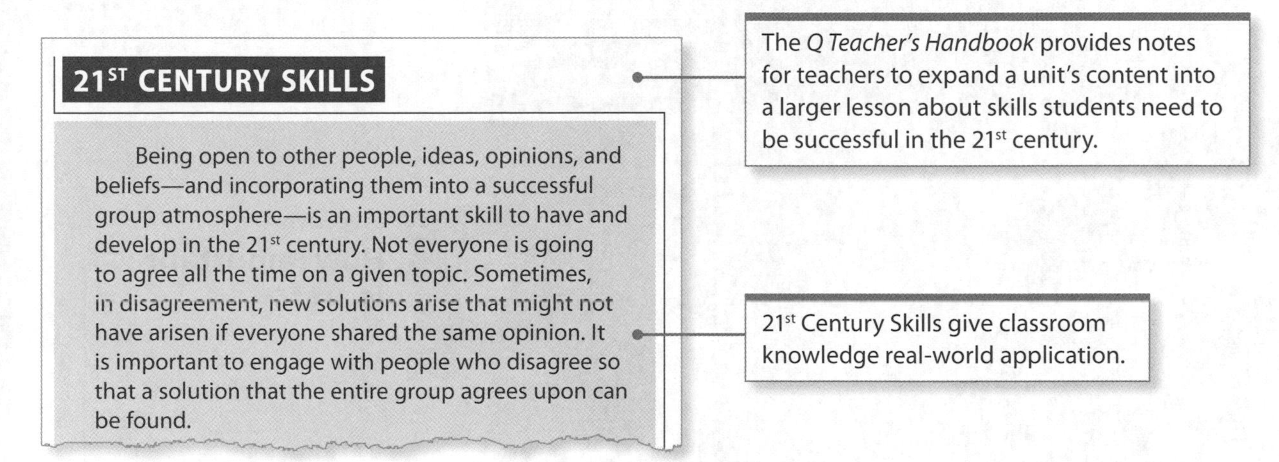

Q ONLINE PRACTICE

Q Online Practice is an online workbook that gives students quick access to all-new content in a range of additional practice activities. The interface is intuitive and user-friendly, allowing students to focus on enhancing their language skills.

For the teacher, *Q Online Practice* includes a digital grade book providing immediate and accurate assessment of each student's progress. Straightforward individual student or class reports can be viewed onscreen, printed, or exported, giving you comprehensive feedback on what students have mastered or where they need more help.

Teacher's Access Code Cards for the digital grade book are available upon adoption or for purchase. Use the access code to register for your *Q Online Practice* account at www.Qonlinepractice.com.

These features of the *Q: Skills for Success* series enable you to help your students develop the skills they need to succeed in their future academic and professional careers. By using learning outcomes, critical thinking, and 21st century skills, you help students gain a deeper knowledge of the material they are presented with, both in and out of the classroom.

QUICKGUIDE

Q connects critical thinking, language skills, and learning outcomes.

LANGUAGE SKILLS

Explicit skills instruction enables students to meet their academic and professional goals.

LEARNING OUTCOMES

Clearly identified **learning outcomes** focus students on the goal of their instruction.

UNIT 5
Art Today

READING compare and contrast organization
VOCABULARY using the dictionary to learn homonyms
WRITING writing a compare and contrast essay
GRAMMAR subordinators and transitions to compare and contrast

LEARNING OUTCOME
Compare and contrast two artists, performers, or works of art that share an interesting relationship.

Unit QUESTION
How important is art?

PREVIEW THE UNIT

A Discuss these questions with your classmates.

What kind of art do you like best: for example, painting, sculpture, music? Why?

Why do people become professional artists? What difficulties do you think artists face?

Look at the photo. What is happening? Why are the people taking pictures?

B Discuss the Unit Question above with your classmates.

Listen to *The Q Classroom*, Track 14 on CD 1, to hear other answers.

104 UNIT 5

105

CRITICAL THINKING

Thought-provoking **unit questions** engage students with the topic and provide a **critical thinking framework** for the unit.

“Having the learning outcome is important because it gives students and teachers a clear idea of what the point of each task/activity in the unit is.”
Lawrence Lawson, Palomar College, California

LANGUAGE SKILLS

Two reading texts provide input on the unit question and give **exposure to academic content.**

What Does It Take to Be a Successful Artist?

1 Why do some artists make it[1]? Why do others fail? Is it possible that successful artists share certain character traits? They probably do. Although they may have different styles and interests, they have a lot in common, too. You can call it what you will: **passion**, drive, **persistence**. The **amateur** rarely has it. The professional artist generally does. It may emerge as fierce ambition or infinite **patience**. The true artist shows a willingness to work hard, no matter what. Time barely matters; only the creative result is important.

Roses and Beetle by Vincent van Gogh

2 For example, when the artist Ralph Fasanella read about a millworkers'[2] strike[3] that happened in Lawrence, Massachusetts in 1912, he decided he had to go there himself to see the town. After arriving, he checked into a cheap hotel, spent the evenings in the

CRITICAL THINKING

Students **discuss** their opinions of each reading text and **analyze** how it changes their perspective on the unit question.

WHAT DO YOU THINK?

A. Discuss the questions in a group. Then choose one question and write one paragraph in response.

1. What qualities does the author of Reading 2 say are needed to become a successful artist? Which of these qualities do you have?
2. Do you agree that artists have to put their art before everything else to achieve greatness? Explain your reasons.

"One of the best features is your focus on developing materials of a high "interest level."

Troy Hammond, Tokyo Gakugei University, International Secondary School, Japan

QUICK GUIDE

Explicit skills instruction prepares students for academic success.

LANGUAGE SKILLS

Explicit instruction and practice in reading, vocabulary, grammar, and writing skills **help students achieve language proficiency.**

LEARNING OUTCOMES

Practice activities allow students to **master the skills** before they are evaluated at the end of the unit.

WHAT DO YOU THINK?

Discuss the questions in a group. Then choose one question and write freely for five to ten minutes in response.

1. What makes someone an artist? Do you think a "real" artist relies more on craft or instinct?
2. When you have to solve a creative problem, do you rely more on craft or inspiration? Why?

Reading Skill Understanding compare and contrast organization

Tip for Success
For information on other common ways of organizing the ideas in a text, look back at the Reading Skill box on page 88.

Writers **compare and contrast** information in order to examine the similarities and differences between two subjects. Comparisons show the subjects' similarities, while contrasts examine their differences. There are many different ways that texts can be organized when writers compare and contrast information. You can use a simple **T-chart** to quickly identify and separate the information about the two subjects. For example, look at the first paragraph of Reading 1 and the chart below.

There are two basic "schools" of songwriting nowadays: one based on craft and the other based on instinct. Craft writers are people who essentially write from nine to five every day, five days a week, whereas instinctive writers work only when they are inspired. Craft writers sometimes say that instinctive writers are "just lucky," while instinctive writers may call craft writers "assembly-line machines." Each approach has its advantages, and each has its problems.

Craft writers	Instinctive writers
write songs every day, from nine to five	write only when they feel inspired
some say craft writers are machines	some say instinctive writers are just lucky

You can also divide the information further by adding categories or topic areas down the side of the chart. (Look at the chart on the top of page 113.) After you chart the information, you can easily examine the ideas for similarities and differences.

112 UNIT 5 | How important is art?

Norah Jones

Their life stories couldn't be more different. Billie Holiday was born in 1915 and had a very difficult life. Her childhood was tough, and she was very poor until she became a successful singer. In contrast, Norah Jones's parents are a famous musician and a dancer, and she was able to attend good schools and colleges. In spite of their different backgrounds, both Holiday and Jones became very successful and famous. Billie Holiday had many hit records, performed concerts at famous venues like Carnegie Hall in New York, and has many songs in the Grammy Hall of Fame. Similarly, Norah Jones's first album, *Come Away with Me*, won eight Grammy Awards, and she has performed concerts in cities all over the world.

Billie Holiday

Because of their different life stories, they had very different musical training. Jones took piano lessons as a child, and studied jazz piano at the University of North Texas. In contrast, Holiday had no musical training. She learned from musicians around her and invented her own unique style of singing. Likewise, Jones had very little formal training as a singer, and learned her way of singing from listening to musicians and recordings, especially Billie Holiday's records.

In many ways, their music, performance style, and abilities are very similar. Both are mainly jazz singers although Nora Jones performs other music as well. Whereas Billie Holiday only sang jazz songs, Jones also sings country and pop songs. Both often sing quiet, emotional songs that are tragic or sad. Nonetheless, Jones also sings some faster pop songs. Finally, Jones and Holiday are both songwriters as well as singers. Jones, however, is better known as a writer than Holiday is.

I love both these singers' music. Billie Holiday's voice is very unusual and beautiful, which is why she is known as one of the best jazz singers ever. Norah Jones also has her own unique singing style, which sometimes surprises me or makes me laugh. Nevertheless, her style of singing reminds me of Billie Holiday. This makes me think that Jones deeply appreciates Holiday as well, and makes me enjoy both of their music even more.

1. What is the thesis statement? Underline it.
2. How is the essay organized? ____________________
3. Why do you think the author organized the essay this way?

____

122 UNIT 5 | How important is art?

> "The tasks are simple, accessible, user-friendly, and very useful."
> *Jessica March, American University of Sharjah, U.A.E.*

LEARNER CENTERED

Q Online Practice provides all new content for additional practice in an easy-to-use online workbook. Every student book includes a ***Q Online Practice* access code card**. Use the access code to register for your *Q Online Practice* account at www.Qonlinepractice.com.

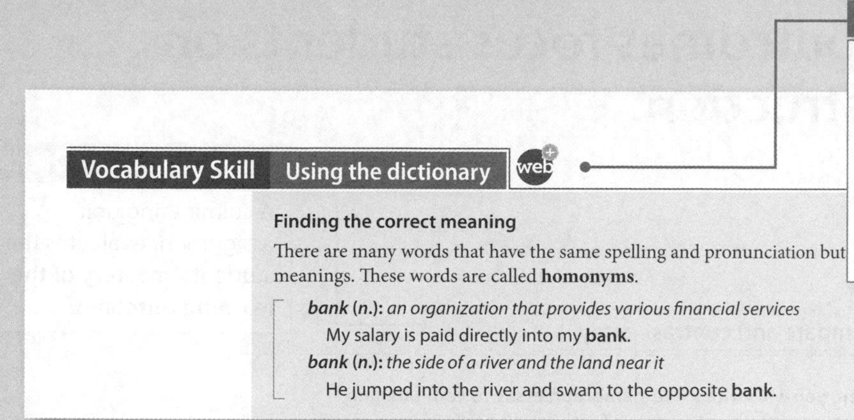

Vocabulary Skill | **Using the dictionary**

Finding the correct meaning

There are many words that have the same spelling and pronunciation but different meanings. These words are called **homonyms**.

bank (*n.*): *an organization that provides various financial services*
My salary is paid directly into my **bank**.
bank (*n.*): *the side of a river and the land near it*
He jumped into the river and swam to the opposite **bank**.

A. Look at the dictionary entry for *craft*. Check (✓) the correct information.

1. *Craft* can be used as:
   - ☐ an adjective
   - ☐ an adverb
   - ☐ a noun
   - ☐ a verb
2. *Craft* can mean:
   - ☐ a boat
   - ☐ a skill
   - ☐ frightening
   - ☐ strange
   - ☐ to make
   - ☐ to give

craft /kræft/ *noun, verb*
• ***noun* 1** [C, U] an activity involving a special skill at making things with your hands: *traditional crafts like basket-weaving* • *a craft fair/workshop* ➲ see also ARTS AND CRAFTS **2** [sing.] all the skills needed for a particular activity: *chefs who learned their craft in five-star hotels* • *the writer's craft* **3** [U] (*formal, disapproving*) skill in making people believe what you want them to believe: *He knew how to win by craft and diplomacy what he could not gain by force.* **4** [C] (*pl.* craft) a boat or ship: *Hundreds of small craft bobbed around the liner as it steamed into the harbor.* • *a landing/pleasure craft* **5** [C] (*pl.* craft) an aircraft or SPACECRAFT
• ***verb*** [usually passive] **~ sth** to make something using special skills, especially with your hands SYN FASHION: *All the furniture is crafted from natural materials.* • *a carefully crafted speech* ➲ see also HANDCRAFTED

All dictionary entries are taken from the *Oxford Advanced American Dictionary for learners of English.*

LANGUAGE SKILLS

A **research-based vocabulary program** focuses students on the words they need to know academically and professionally, using skill strategies based on the same research as the Oxford dictionaries.

All dictionary entries are taken from the *Oxford Advanced American Dictionary for learners of English*.

The ***Oxford Advanced American Dictionary for learners of English*** was developed with English learners in mind, and provides extra learning tools for pronunciation, verb types, basic grammar structures, and more.

The Oxford 3000™
The Oxford 3000 encompasses **the 3000 most important words to learn in English.** It is based on a comprehensive analysis of the Oxford English Corpus, a two-billion word collection of English text, and on extensive research with both language and pedagogical experts.

The Academic Word List AWL
The Academic Word List was created by Averil Coxhead and contains **570 words that are commonly used in academic English,** such as in textbooks or articles across a wide range of academic subject areas. These words are a great place to start if you are studying English for academic purposes.

Clear learning outcomes focus students on the goals of instruction.

LEARNING OUTCOMES

A culminating unit assignment evaluates the students' **mastery of the learning outcome.**

Unit Assignment Write a compare and contrast essay

In this assignment, you will write a five-paragraph essay to compare and contrast two artists, performers, or works of art. As you prepare your essay, think about the Unit Question, "How important is art?" and refer to the Self-Assessment checklist on page 128. Use information from Readings 1 and 2 and your work in this unit to support your ideas.

For alternative unit assignments, see the *Q: Skills for Success Teacher's Handbook*.

PLAN AND WRITE

A. BRAINSTORM Follow these steps to help you gather ideas for your essay. Write your ideas in your notebook.

1. Work with a partner. Brainstorm ideas for the topic of your essay. You can choose two artists (such as painters, musicians, or writers) or two works of art (such as paintings, songs, books, poems, or movies). Choose pairs of subjects that you think have an interesting or important relationship to each other.

LEARNER CENTERED

Track Your Success allows students to **assess their own progress** and provides guidance on remediation.

Check (✓) the skills you learned. If you need more work on a skill, refer to the page(s) in parentheses.

READING	I can understand compare and contrast organization. (p. 112)
VOCABULARY	I can use a dictionary to understand the meanings of homonyms. (p. 119)
WRITING	I can write a compare and contrast essay. (p. 121)
GRAMMAR	I can use subordinators and transitions to compare and contrast. (p. 124)
LEARNING OUTCOME	I can compare and contrast two artists, performers, or works of art that share an interesting relationship.

“Students can check their learning . . . and they can focus on the essential points when they study.”

Suh Yoomi, Seoul, South Korea

Q Online Practice

For the student

- **Easy-to-use:** a simple interface allows students to focus on enhancing their reading and writing skills, not learning a new software program
- **Flexible:** for use anywhere there's an Internet connection
- **Access code card:** a *Q Online Practice* access code is included with the student book. Use the access code to register for *Q Online Practice* at www.Qonlinepractice.com

For the teacher

- **Simple yet powerful:** automatically grades student exercises and tracks progress
- **Straightforward:** online management system to review, print, or export reports
- **Flexible:** for use in the classroom or easily assigned as homework
- **Access code card:** contact your sales rep for your *Q Online Practice* teacher's access code

Teacher Resources

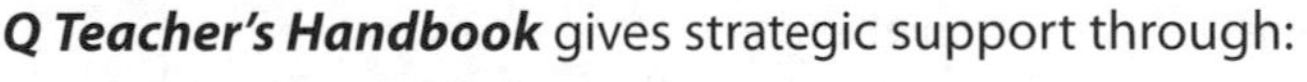

Q Teacher's Handbook gives strategic support through:

- specific teaching notes for each activity
- ideas for ensuring student participation
- multilevel strategies and expansion activities
- the answer key
- special sections on 21st century skills and critical thinking
- a ***Testing Program CD-ROM*** with a customizable test for each unit

Oxford Teachers' Club

For additional resources visit the *Q: Skills for Success* companion website at www.oup.com/elt/teacher/Qskillsforsuccess

Q Class Audio includes:

- reading texts
- *The Q Classroom*

> "It's an interesting, engaging series which provides plenty of materials that are easy to use in class, as well as instructionally promising."
> *Donald Weasenforth, Collin College, Texas*

UNIT	READING	WRITING
1 Power and Responsibility **Q What makes someone a hero?** **READING 1: We All Need a Hero** A Book Excerpt (Cultural Anthropology) **READING 2: Everyday People Changing the World** An Online Article (Education and Social Issues)	• Read subheadings to anticipate content of a reading • Complete a chart to capture main ideas • Preview text and predict what a text is about using a variety of strategies • Read for main ideas • Read for details • Use glosses and footnotes to aid comprehension • Read and recognize different text types	• Develop a paragraph: topic sentence, supporting sentences, and concluding sentence • Write an analysis paragraph • Plan before writing • Make an outline • Revise, edit, and rewrite • Give feedback to peers and self-assess
2 Appearances **Q What makes you want to buy something?** **READING 1: So Much Dead Space** An Article from a Professional Publication (Psychology and Business) **READING 2: Now on Stage: Your Home!** A Magazine Article (Design and Marketing)	• Annotate and highlight a text to identify important ideas • Use a graphic organizer to understand reasons • Preview text using a variety of strategies • Read for main ideas • Read for details • Use glosses and footnotes to aid comprehension • Read and recognize different text types	• Use adjectives, sensory language, and details to create descriptive language • Write a descriptive essay • Plan before writing • Make an outline • Revise, edit, and rewrite • Give feedback to peers and self-assess
3 Growing Up **Q What important lessons do we learn as children?** **READING 1: The Good Teen** A News Magazine Article (Developmental Psychology) **READING 2: *Bird by Bird*** A Memoir Excerpt (Writing)	• Locate specific information in a text to understand context better • Make inferences to improve comprehension and understand a text more deeply • Preview text using a variety of strategies • Read for main ideas • Read for details • Use glosses and footnotes to aid comprehension • Read and recognize different text types	• Use time words and clauses to express the order of events • Write a narrative essay with an introduction, body, and conclusion • Plan before writing • Make an outline • Revise, edit, and rewrite • Give feedback to peers and self-assess

VOCABULARY	GRAMMAR	CRITICAL THINKING	UNIT OUTCOME
• Use the dictionary to expand vocabulary • Match definitions • Define new terms • Learn selected vocabulary words from the Oxford 3000 and the Academic Word List	• Restrictive relative clauses	• Explain ideas to demonstrate comprehension • Compare information using a chart • Support opinions with reasons and examples • Reflect on the unit question • Connect ideas across texts or readings • Express ideas/reactions/ opinions orally and in writing • Apply unit tips and use *Q Online Practice* to become a strategic learner	• Analyze the qualities that make a person a hero and provide examples of the accomplishments of heroes.
• Recognize collocations with nouns in order to learn patterns of usage • Match definitions • Define new terms • Learn selected vocabulary words from the Oxford 3000 and the Academic Word List	• Definite and indefinite articles	• Discuss questions in a group to clarify understanding of new material • Apply new information to your own experience • Reflect on the unit question • Connect ideas across texts or readings • Express ideas/reactions/ opinions orally and in writing • Apply unit tips and use *Q Online Practice* to become a strategic learner	• Describe aspects of a product or service to make someone want to purchase or use it.
• Build vocabulary using prefixes and suffixes • Match definitions • Define new terms • Learn selected vocabulary words from the Oxford 3000 and the Academic Word List	• Past perfect	• Relate information to your own experience to remember and understand it better • Reflect on the unit question • Connect ideas across texts or readings • Express ideas/reactions/ opinions orally and in writing • Apply unit tips and use *Q Online Practice* to become a strategic learner	• Relate a personal memory of someone or something that influenced you when you were younger.

UNIT	READING	WRITING
4 Health **Q How does the environment affect our health?** **READING 1: Can Climate Change Make Us Sicker?** A Newspaper Article (Health and Public Policy) **READING 2: Tips for a Greener Planet: And a Happier, Healthier You** An Online Article (Consumer Tips)	• Understand purpose and types of organization patterns to read more critically • Preview text using a variety of strategies • Read for main ideas • Read for details • Use glosses and footnotes to aid comprehension • Read and recognize different text types	• Identify hooks, thesis statements, and topic sentences • Write a five-paragraph problem and solution essay • Plan before writing • Make an outline • Revise, edit, and rewrite • Give feedback to peers and self-assess
5 Art Today **Q How important is art?** **READING 1: Two Styles of Songwriting** A Book Excerpt (Music and Writing) **READING 2: What Does It Take to Be a Successful Artist?** A Book Excerpt (Art)	• Locate specific information in a text to understand main ideas • Use compare and contrast organization to examine similarities and differences between two subjects • Preview text using a variety of strategies • Read for main ideas • Read for details • Use glosses and footnotes to aid comprehension • Read and recognize different text types	• Identify patterns of organization in compare and contrast essays • Write a five-paragraph compare and contrast essay • Plan before writing • Make an outline • Revise, edit, and rewrite • Give feedback to peers and self-assess
6 The Science of Food **Q Should science influence what we eat?** **READING 1: Eating Well: Less Science, More Common Sense** A Magazine Article (Nutrition and Diet) **READING 2: Anatomy of a Nutrition Trend** An Online Magazine Article (Marketing and Sociology)	• Recognize a writer's bias to better evaluate his or her ideas • Preview text using a variety of strategies • Read for main ideas • Read for details • Use glosses and footnotes to aid comprehension • Read and recognize different text types	• Identify patterns of organization in a cause and effect essay • Write a five-paragraph cause and effect essay • Plan before writing • Make an outline • Revise, edit, and rewrite • Give feedback to peers and self-assess

VOCABULARY	GRAMMAR	CRITICAL THINKING	UNIT OUTCOME
• Learn synonyms to expand your vocabulary and add variety to your writing and speaking • Match definitions • Define new terms • Learn selected vocabulary words from the Oxford 3000 and the Academic Word List	• Real conditionals	• Anticipate problems and propose solutions • Use charts to clarify the relationships between ideas and to focus on main points • Reflect on the unit question • Connect ideas across texts or readings • Express ideas/reactions/ opinions orally and in writing • Apply unit tips and use *Q Online Practice* to become a strategic learner	• Identify and describe a harmful environmental issue and propose a possible solution to the problem.
• Use the dictionary to distinguish between homonyms • Match definitions • Define new terms • Learn selected vocabulary words from the Oxford 3000 and the Academic Word List	• Subordinators and transitions to compare and contrast	• Use a chart to categorize similarities and differences • Support your opinion with reasons and examples • Reflect on the unit question • Connect ideas across texts or readings • Express ideas/reactions/ opinions orally and in writing • Apply unit tips and use *Q Online Practice* to become a strategic learner	• Compare and contrast two artists, performers, or works of art that share an interesting relationship.
• Use collocations with prepositions to express cause and effect • Match definitions • Define new terms • Learn selected vocabulary words from the Oxford 3000 and the Academic Word List	• Agents with the passive voice	• Apply information to your own life • Compare and contrast trends in different fields • Use a T-chart to analyze cause and effect • Reflect on the unit question • Connect ideas across texts or readings • Express ideas/reactions/ opinions orally and in writing • Apply unit tips and use *Q Online Practice* to become a strategic learner	• Express your opinions about the positive or negative effects of science on the food we eat.

UNIT	READING	WRITING
7 Work and Education **Q Does school prepare you for work?** **READING 1: From Student to Employee** A Magazine Article (Education and Business) **READING 2: Making My First Post-College Decision** A Blog Posting (Careers)	• Locate specific information in a text • Use an outline to understand how a text is organized and to aid study • Preview text using a variety of strategies • Read for main ideas • Read for details • Use glosses and footnotes to aid comprehension • Read and recognize different text types	• Compare two summaries • Write a summary • Plan before writing • Make an outline • Revise, edit, and rewrite • Give feedback to peers and self-assess
8 Discovery **Q Is discovery always a good thing?** **READING 1: A Tribe Is Discovered** A Newspaper Article (Anthropology) **READING 2: The Kipunji** Online Articles (Zoology)	• Understand the purpose of quoted speech • Distinguish fact from opinion • Preview text using a variety of strategies • Read for main ideas • Read for details • Use glosses and footnotes to aid comprehension • Read and recognize different text types	• Summarize information from an opinion essay • Write a five-paragraph opinion essay • Plan before writing • Make an outline • Revise, edit, and rewrite • Give feedback to peers and self-assess
9 Humans and Nature **Q Have humans lost their connection to nature?** **READING 1: Survival School** A Newspaper Article (Narrative) **READING 2: Man Against Nature** A Newspaper Article (Suburban Ecology)	• Identify sources of information • Take episodic notes on a narrative • Preview text using a variety of strategies • Read for main ideas • Read for details • Use glosses and footnotes to aid comprehension • Read and recognize different text types	• Use different types of sentence types (passive, reported speech, etc.) to add variety to your writing • Write a five-paragraph narrative essay • Plan before writing • Make an outline • Revise, edit, and rewrite • Give feedback to peers and self-assess
10 Child's Play **Q Why is it important to play?** **READING 1: The Promise of Play** A Book Excerpt (Psychology) **READING 2: Child's Play: It's Not Just for Fun** An Article (Child Development)	• Identify counterarguments and refutations to better evaluate ideas in a text • Complete a chart to capture main ideas • Preview text using a variety of strategies • Read for main ideas • Read for details • Use glosses and footnotes to aid comprehension • Read and recognize different text types	• Understand the elements of a persuasive essay • Write a five-paragraph persuasive essay • Plan before writing • Make an outline • Revise, edit, and rewrite • Give feedback to peers and self-assess

VOCABULARY	GRAMMAR	CRITICAL THINKING	UNIT OUTCOME
• Learn to recognize different word forms to expand your vocabulary • Match definitions • Define new terms • Learn selected vocabulary words from the Oxford 3000 and the Academic Word List	• Reported speech with the present tense	• Justify your opinions • Apply and compare new information to your own experience • Evaluate advantages and disadvantages of a situation • Reflect on the unit question • Connect ideas across texts or readings • Express ideas/reactions/ opinions orally and in writing • Apply unit tips and use *Q Online Practice* to become a strategic learner	• Summarize important points of a text by paraphrasing the author's purpose, thesis statement, main ideas, and conclusions.
• Use word roots to understand the meaning of unfamiliar words • Match definitions • Define new terms • Learn selected vocabulary words from the Oxford 3000 and the Academic Word List	• Adverb phrases of reason	• Assess benefits and risks of an action • Synthesize information from texts and your experience • Reflect on the unit question • Evaluate and reach consensus on a candidate's work • Connect ideas across texts or readings • Express ideas/reactions/ opinions orally and in writing • Apply unit tips and use *Q Online Practice* to become a strategic learner	• State and defend your opinion about whether a specific discovery or type of exploration is a good or bad thing.
• Recognize metaphoric language • Match definitions • Define new terms • Learn selected vocabulary words from the Oxford 3000 and the Academic Word List	• Parallel structure and ellipsis	• Make a decision based on careful examination of information • Reflect on the unit question • Connect ideas across texts or readings • Express ideas/reactions/ opinions orally and in writing • Apply unit tips and use *Q Online Practice* to become a strategic learner	• Relate a story about how people connect with nature in a positive or negative way.
• Use collocations with prepositions to expand vocabulary and improve fluency • Match definitions • Define new terms • Learn selected vocabulary words from the Oxford 3000 and the Academic Word List	• Adverb clauses of concession	• Hypothesize what another person might think or do • Understand opposing points of view • Use a chart to understand the connections between ideas • Reflect on the unit question • Connect ideas across texts or readings • Express ideas/reactions/ opinions orally and in writing • Apply unit tips and use *Q Online Practice* to become a strategic learner	• Make arguments to persuade readers that video games are helpful or harmful to children.

UNIT 1

Unit QUESTION

What makes someone a hero?

Power and Responsibility

READING • previewing and predicting
VOCABULARY • using the dictionary
WRITING • writing a well-structured paragraph
GRAMMAR • restrictive relative clauses

LEARNING OUTCOME

Analyze the qualities that make a person a hero and provide examples of the accomplishments of heroes.

Reading and Writing 4, pages 2–3

Preview the Unit

Learning Outcome

1. Ask for a volunteer to read the unit skills and the unit Learning Outcome.
2. Explain: *This is what you are expected to be able to do by the unit's end. The Learning Outcome explains how you are going to be evaluated. With this outcome in mind, you should focus on learning those skills (Reading, Vocabulary, Writing, Grammar) that will support your goal of analyzing what makes someone a hero. You can also act as a mentor in the classroom to help your classmates learn the skills and meet this Learning Outcome.*

Cultural Background Note

Explain that in American popular culture, superheroes are characters with special or superhuman powers and are dedicated to protecting people from villains. Their costumes have colors or symbols that represent who they are. Superheroes first appeared in comic books, but now their stories are told in movies, and you can see superheroes on products from T-shirts to toothbrushes.

A (15 minutes)

1. Ask students to name any superheroes they know (Superman, Batman, Spider-Man, etc.). Ask: *What makes these superheroes special?*
2. Put students in pairs or small groups to discuss the first two questions.
3. Call on volunteers to share their ideas with the class. Ask: *Do heroes need to have special powers? Who are some heroes you've heard about in the news?*
4. Focus students' attention on the photo. Have a volunteer describe the photo to the class. Read the third question aloud. Elicit students' answers.

Preview the Unit A Answers, p. 3

Answers will vary. Sample answers:

1. People of all ages like superheroes because they admire what superheroes do and how they help others.
2. My aunt is my hero because she has had many challenges in her life, but she always does what's best for her family.
3. This person is showing heroism because he's overcoming a challenge, his physical disability, to achieve success.

B (15 minutes)

1. Introduce the Unit Question: "What makes someone a hero?" Explain that each unit in Q focuses on a Unit Question that students will consider throughout the unit and discuss in their Unit Assignment. Ask related information questions or questions about personal experience to help students prepare for answering the more abstract Unit Question. For example ask: *What qualities do real heroes have? What kind of people are heroes?*
2. Put students in small groups and give each group a piece of poster paper and a marker.
3. Read the Unit Question aloud. Give students a minute to silently consider their answers to the question. Tell students to pass the paper and the marker around the group. Direct each group member to write a different answer to the question. Encourage them to help one another.

4. Ask each group to choose a reporter to read the group's answers to the class. Point out similarities and differences among the answers. If answers from different groups are similar, make a group list that incorporates the answers. Post the list to refer to later in the unit.

Preview the Unit B Answers, p. 3
Answers will vary. Sample answers:
Lower-level answer: *A hero helps people.*
On-level answer: *A hero does great things in dangerous situations.*
Higher-level answer: *To me, a hero is someone who helps other people, especially in difficult or dangerous situations.*

The Q Classroom (5 minutes)

CD1, Track 2

1. Play *The Q Classroom.* Use the example from the audio to help students continue the conversation. Ask: *How did the students answer the question? Do you agree or disagree with their ideas? Why?*
2. Say: *The students in the audio mention several examples of heroes* (firefighters; soldiers; people who fight injustice; someone who helps others in a disaster; a surgeon). *In your opinion, which of these people is most heroic? Why?*

Reading and Writing 4, page 4

C (10 minutes)

1. Ask for a volunteer to read the directions. Discuss the first quotation as a class. Ask students what the quotation means and if they agree.
2. Direct students to complete the activity with a partner. Call on volunteers to share their ideas.

MULTILEVEL OPTION

Provide lower-level students with paraphrases of the quotations: *There's a hero in all of us who gives us strength; The only difference between a hero and an ordinary man is that a hero is braver for longer; People who recover from the mistakes they've made are heroes; You can't be a hero unless you care about people.* Instruct students to match each quotation to the correct paraphrase. This will provide them with additional language to discuss their ideas.

Preview the Unit C Answers, p. 4
Answers will vary. Sample answers:
1. There is a hero inside each person.
2. A hero is patient as well as brave.
3. Heroes are people who learn from their mistakes.
4. You must care about other people to be a hero.

D (10 minutes)

1. Direct students to read the directions and complete the chart individually.
2. Have students compare their chart with a partner. Tell them to look back at their answers to the Unit Question when discussing the qualities of a hero.
3. Draw the chart and elicit ideas from volunteers.

Preview the Unit D Answers, p. 4
Answers will vary. Sample answers:
Qualities of a hero: brave, courageous, strong, smart
Qualities of an ordinary person: afraid, weak, impatient

READING

Reading and Writing 4, page 5

READING 1: We All Need a Hero

VOCABULARY (15 minutes)

1. Read the first sentence aloud and elicit guesses about what *embody* means. Then find the correct definition.
2. Direct students to read each sentence, guess what the bold word means, and write the word next to the correct definition.
3. Have students compare answers with a partner. Elicit answers from volunteers. Discuss any context clues that helped students understand the meanings of the words.
4. Say each vocabulary word and have students repeat. Highlight the syllable in each word that receives primary stress.

Vocabulary Answers, pp. 5–6
a. acknowledged for;
b. resolve;
c. inherently;
d. aspire to;
e. constrained;
f. adversity;
g. achievement;
h. confront;
i. embody;
j. inclined to;
k. version;
l. pursue

For additional practice with the vocabulary, have students visit *Q Online Practice.*

Reading and Writing 4, page 6

Reading Skill: Previewing and predicting (10 minutes)

1. Read the information about previewing and predicting.
2. Check comprehension by asking questions: *What three things should you do when you preview a text?* As students answer the question, you may want to list the three steps on a piece of poster paper so students can always refer to them.

Tip for Success (1 minute)

1. Read the tip aloud. Explain to students that research papers may require them to use 10, or even 20, sources.
2. Ask students to imagine how long it would take them to read all those books and articles compared to how long it would take just to preview them. This tip is a great time-saver!

PREVIEW READING 1

A (5 minutes)

1. Have a volunteer read the introduction aloud. Direct students to write their predictions.
2. Have students check their predictions after reading.

Preview Reading 1 Activity A Answers, p. 6

Answers will vary. Sample answers:

1. The text will be about real heroes, like policemen.
2. The text will be about fictional superheroes.

21ST CENTURY SKILLS

Employers want employees who can manage their time well. Previewing a text and making predictions about its content will help students be more efficient in the classroom as well as in the workplace. Provide an example of how previewing might help students in their jobs. For example, if their e-mail inbox has 30 unread messages, they can preview the emails by noting the senders and subject lines in order to determine which messages are the most urgent and should be read first. This will save time and allow them to focus on the issues that need attention right away.

Encourage students to preview a wide range of texts, from textbook chapters to email messages, to help them predict the content of a text, prioritize what they need to read, and manage their time.

Reading and Writing 4, page 7

B (5 minutes)

1. Direct students to complete the activity and then compare answers with a partner.
2. Tell students to review their answers after they have finished reading.

Preview Reading 1 Activity B Answers, p. 7

Students may check either answer. The correct ideas are:

1. The qualities of superheroes
2. How superheroes can inspire us
3. Why superheroes give us courage
4. How superheroes can set an example

For additional practice with previewing and predicting, have students visit *Q Online Practice.*

Reading 1 Background Note

Superman is known for his cape, which has the letter "S" on it for his name. Superman's secret identity is Clark Kent, a reporter. His powers include X-ray vision, flight, and superhuman strength.

Batman is the secret identity of Bruce Wayne, who pledged to fight crime after his parents were murdered when he was a child. Though Batman does not have superpowers, he makes use of his intelligence and technology.

Spiderman is the alter ego of Peter Parker. He has superhuman strength, the ability to heal quickly, and the ability to shoot strong spider webs from his wrists. He also has a "spider sense," which allows him to respond quickly to dangerous situations.

READ (20 minutes)

CD1, Track 3

1. Instruct students to read the excerpt. Point out the glossed words in the excerpt and show students how to use each number to refer to these words as they read.
2. When students have finished reading, answer any questions they may have about the excerpt or additional vocabulary.
3. Play the audio and have students follow along.

Reading and Writing 4, page 9

MAIN IDEAS (5 minutes)

1. Remind students that the main ideas are the most important ideas in the text.
2. Tell students to read the main ideas and number them in the order they are developed. Tell them to refer back to the text and underline each main idea as they find it.
3. Elicit the answers from volunteers.

Main Ideas Answers, p. 9

a. 4; **b.** 5; **c.** 1; **d.** 3; **e.** 2

DETAILS (10 minutes)

1. Direct students to answer the questions.
2. Have students compare answers with a partner. Remind them to look back at the excerpt to check their answers.
3. Go over the answers with the class.

Details Answers, pp. 9–10

1. They represent our highest ambitions and help us deal with our worst nightmares.
2. No. Some have normal abilities that they have developed to a superhuman level.
3. He believed that good is inherently attractive.
4. Superhero stories have been popular for so long because they speak to our hopes.
5. When we face adversity, we are inclined to give up.
6. Batman can teach us to keep on going even when the going is tough.

For additional practice with reading comprehension, have students visit *Q Online Practice*.

Reading and Writing 4, page 10

WHAT DO YOU THINK? (20 minutes)

1. Ask students to read the questions and reflect on their answers.
2. Seat students in small groups and assign roles: a group leader to make sure everyone contributes, a note-taker to record the group's ideas, a reporter to share the group's ideas with the class, and a timekeeper to watch the clock.
3. Give students five minutes to discuss the questions. Call time if conversations are winding down. Allow them an extra minute or two if necessary.
4. Call on each group's reporter to share ideas with the class.
5. Have each student choose one of the questions and write for 5–10 minutes in response.
6. Call on volunteers to share their responses.

MULTILEVEL OPTION:

Pair lower-level students and have them choose the same question to respond to.

As higher-level students finish, they can share their responses with a partner. Alternatively, higher-level students can be paired with lower-level students, so that they can share their ideas and help lower-level students with vocabulary or expressions.

What Do You Think? Activity Answers, p. 10

Answers will vary. Sample answers:

1. Yes, if I could have a superpower I would want one. It would be amazing to be able to fly.
2. I think this statement is suggesting that just because someone has special powers, it doesn't mean they are a hero. It's what they do with their powers that makes them a hero.
3. One superhero that I know is the mother from The Incredibles. She inspires me because she is a superhero who fights crime, but she also has a regular life and takes care of her family.

Critical Thinking Tip (1 minute)

1. Read the tip aloud.
2. Explain: It's important to use your own words to explain a quotation. If you don't, you will need to use quotation marks.

EXPANSION ACTIVITY: Hero Poster (15 minutes)

1. Expand on the What Do You Think? questions by having students make a poster of an imaginary superhero and his/her powers.
2. Working in small groups, students should brainstorm the hero's super powers and how he/she inspires people.
3. Each group should design a poster that describes their superhero. It should include a picture and a description of the hero's super powers. It should also include some quotations from people about how the hero inspires them.
4. Have groups present their posters to the class.

Learning Outcome

Use the Learning Outcome to frame the purpose and relevance of Reading 1. Ask: *What did you learn from Reading 1 that prepares you to analyze what makes a person a hero and provide examples of that hero's accomplishments?* (Students read about the qualities of superheroes and how they inspire us to do good and help us deal with our fears. They may want to use some of these ideas when they write their analysis paragraph for the Unit Assignment.)

READING 2: Heroes in Real Life

VOCABULARY (15 minutes)

1. Read the directions aloud and do the first item together as a class.
2. Direct students to work with a partner to complete the activity.
3. Elicit the answers from volunteers. Pronounce each vocabulary word and have students repeat. Highlight the syllable that receives primary stress in each word.

Vocabulary Answers, pp. 10–11

These definitions are incorrect:

1. too much of something;
2. the best;
3. a test of ability;
4. lowest;
5. to prevent someone from using something;
6. salary to an employee;
7. to do something in the usual way;
8. to see something from a distance;
9. a loud noise;
10. people who take things apart;
11. to make something easy;
12. a type of illness

web+ For additional practice with the vocabulary, have students visit *Q Online Practice.*

Reading and Writing 4, page 11

PREVIEW READING 2 (10 minutes)

1. Ask: *Do you remember what to do when you preview a text?* (Read the title, look at the images, read any subheadings.)
2. Read the introduction aloud. Direct students to preview the articles and write their predictions.
3. Tell students they should review their predictions after reading the text.

Reading 2 Background Note

As a child, Yohannes Gebregeorgis was taught to read by Peace Corps Volunteers. His organization, *Ethiopia Reads*, seeks to build a culture of reading in Ethiopia by connecting children to books. *Ethiopia Reads* builds libraries, publishes books in Ethiopian languages, and trains educators to foster a love for books among their students.

Reading and Writing 4, page 12

READ (20 minutes)

CD1, Track 4

1. Instruct students to read the article. Remind them to refer to the glossed words as they read.
2. When students have finished reading, answer any questions they may have about the articles or additional vocabulary.
3. Play the audio and have students follow along.

Reading and Writing 4, page 15

MAIN IDEAS (15 minutes)

1. Read the directions aloud. Remind students to look back at the articles for the information to fill in the chart.
2. Ask students to complete the chart individually.
3. Call on students to share their answers.

Main Ideas Answers, p. 15

1. Home country: Argentina
2. Job: children's librarian
3. Reason for interest in cause: ...he realized the impact children's books could make on a child's sense of wonder and vision; ...noticed a lot of trash outside the school.
4. First things he/she did: He wrote *Silly Mammo*, which was the first bilingual Amharic-English children's book; They began volunteering with a government program, collecting waste in the area.
5. Organization: Ethiopia Reads in 1988; Esperanza de Vida in 1997;
6. Mission: To bring children's libraries to Ethiopia; To organize and lead young participants in "making our streets and our environment cleaner."
7. Major accomplishment: In 2002, he opened the Shola Children's Library in Addis Ababa; ...about 60 bags of trash for recycling.

Reading and Writing 4, page 16

DETAILS (15 minutes)

1. Direct students to correct the false statements.
2. Have students compare answers with a partner. Remind them look back at the article to check their answers.
3. Go over the answers with the class.

Details Answers, p. 16

1. He thinks the books that students read outside of school are the "spices of education."
2. He wrote Silly Mammo because he was unable to find any Ethiopian books.
3. When the Shola Children's Library opened, young readers overwhelmed his home.
4. He believes that literacy and education will free his impoverished land.
5. The Jujuy province is an area known for its rich culture and spectacular vistas.
6. Her organization's efforts have expanded beyond the immediate area.
7. On Saturdays, the group hikes into the mountains, where they work for hours.
8. The local government helps to transport the recyclables to the drop-off center.

For additional practice with reading comprehension, have students visit *Q Online Practice*.

WHAT DO YOU THINK?

A (15 minutes)

1. Ask students to read the questions and reflect on their answers.
2. Seat students in small groups and assign roles: a group leader to make sure everyone contributes, a note-taker to record the group's ideas, a reporter to share the group's ideas with the class, and a timekeeper to watch the clock.
3. Give students five minutes to discuss the questions. Call time if conversations are winding down. Allow them an extra minute or two if necessary.
4. Call on each group's reporter to share ideas with the class.
5. Direct students to choose one question and write a paragraph in response.
6. Call on volunteers to share their responses.

What Do You Think? Activity A Answers, pp. 16–17

Answers will vary. Sample answers:

1. Yes, I volunteered to pick up trash in my neighborhood park.
2. I think police officers are seen as heroes because they help to keep us safe and enforce the laws. Also, teachers are viewed as heroes for their work with children.
3. Someone in the news who is a real-life hero is the rescuer who went underground to rescue the thirty-three miners in Chile. He was a very brave man.

Critical Q: Expansion Activity

Explain Your Ideas

Point out to students that question 2 on p. 16 asks them *Why?*, which means they should explain their answer with reasons. Explain that they will want to give valid reasons that are based on facts or on their own experiences.

Ask volunteers to share their answers to the question. Write the answers on the board and add bullet points with their reasons. Ask them if their reasons were based on something in the reading or on their own experiences.

Reading and Writing 4, page 17

B (10 minutes)

1. Tell the students that they should think about both Reading 1 and Reading 2 as they answer the questions in Activity B.
2. Call on each group to share their ideas.

What Do You Think? Activity B Answers, p. 17

Answers will vary. Sample answers:

1. Real-life heroes are like superheroes because they do things that other people don't normally do. They help people in difficult or dangerous situations. / Real-life heroes are different from superheroes because they don't have superpowers, such as the ability to fly.
2. I would rather be a real-life hero because superheroes only exist in our imagination. Real-life heroes help people in dangerous or difficult situations.

Learning Outcome

Use the Learning Outcome to frame the purpose and relevance of Readings 1 and 2. Ask: *What did you learn from Readings 1 and 2 that prepares you to analyze what makes a person a hero and provide examples of that hero's accomplishments?* (Students learned what both superheroes and real-life heroes do. They may want to use information from the readings when they write their analysis paragraphs.)

Vocabulary Skill: Using the dictionary (10 minutes)

1. Ask a volunteer to read the information about a dictionary entry.
2. Check comprehension: *What information does a dictionary entry include? How many syllables does* embody *have? What are some synonyms for* embody*? Is this information useful when learning a new word?*

Skill Note

Knowing a word is much more complex than just knowing its definition. More advanced students realize the importance of learning multiple things about a word, such as its pronunciation, other words that it's used with (collocations), its part of speech, its level of formality, etc. Many words have different meanings depending on the context, which is why multiple definitions are useful. Encourage students to pay attention to these details as they look up new vocabulary words in the dictionary.

A (15 minutes)

1. Read the directions aloud and direct students to complete the activity individually.
2. Go over the answers with the class.

Vocabulary Skill A Answers, p. 17

The following points are checked: syllable division; pronunciation; part(s) of speech; spelling of word endings; example sentences; synonyms; common collocation(s)

Reading and Writing 4, page 18

Tip for Success (1 minute)

1. Read the tip aloud.
2. Explain: *When you record information about a word, use the abbreviations* –sth *and* –sb. *Using the abbreviations will save you time and help you remember what they mean.*

B (15 minutes)

1. Have students complete the activity individually and then compare answers with a partner.
2. Elicit answers from volunteers.

Vocabulary Skill B Answers, pp. 18–19

1. five;
2. face up to;
3. be confronted with sth;
4. inherent: adjective; inherently: adverb;
5. intrinsic;
6. in / her / ent / ly;
7. the passive;
8. three;
9. to and from;
10. a / chieve / ment;
11. two;
12. a sense of achievement

Reading and Writing 4, page 19

C (10 minutes)

1. Have students work with a partner to complete the activity. Remind them to use the questions in Activity B as an example.
2. Have volunteers share any information they learned about the words they looked up.

MULTILEVEL OPTION

For Activity C, you can pre-select the words and assign them to students depending on their level.

Vocabulary Skill C Answers, p. 19

Answers will vary.

For additional practice with using the dictionary, have students visit *Q Online Practice.*

Reading and Writing 4, page 20

WRITING

Writing Skill: Writing a well-structured paragraph (10 minutes)

1. Direct students to read the information about the parts of a paragraph.
2. Check comprehension: *What does a topic sentence do? How does it help the reader? How can you create unity with supporting sentences? How can you create coherence? What does a concluding sentence do?*

Tip for Success (1 minute)

1. Read the tip aloud.
2. Explain to students that they can use this tip in the outline stage of their writing. Remind them of this when they plan their Unit Assignment in Activity B on p. 25.

A (15 minutes)

1. Ask for volunteers to read the paragraph aloud.
2. Then direct students to follow the steps on p. 21 to identify the parts of the paragraph.
3. Elicit answers from volunteers. You may want to project the paragraph to go over the answers.

Writing Skill A Answers, p. 21

1. Successful people share three common qualities (that allow them to stand out).
2. They also work longer hours.
3. Circle: First, Second, Finally
4. a; This sentence summarizes the whole paragraph and restates the topic.

Reading and Writing 4, page 21

B (10 minutes)

1. Direct students to work with a partner to complete the activity. Tell them to review the information on p. 20 if they need help.
2. Elicit answers from volunteers.

Writing Skill B Answers, p. 21

a. 2;	**b.** 4;	**c.** 1;	**d.** 3;
e. 8;	**f.** 6;	**g.** 7;	**h.** 5

web For additional practice with writing a well-structured paragraph, have students visit *Q Online Practice*.

Reading and Writing 4, page 22

Grammar: Restrictive relative clauses (15 minutes)

1. Ask volunteers to read the information about restrictive relative clauses and the examples.
2. Explain that the relative clauses are "restrictive" because they give essential information about nouns or help identify them.
3. Check comprehension by asking questions:
What do restrictive relative clauses do?
Which relative pronouns do we use for people?
Which relative pronouns do we use for things?
When can you omit the relative pronoun?

Skill Note

If students have difficulty recognizing restrictive relative clauses, remind them that they describe or identify nouns. A relative clause is restrictive when it is necessary to identify the noun; it does not merely give additional information about it. For example, the restrictive relative clause in the sentence "A superhero helps people who cannot help themselves" tells which kind of people superheroes help.

To help students recognize restrictive relative clauses, teach them how to identify the noun or noun phrase. Then, have them look at the relative clause to decide if it describes or identifies the noun.

Reading and Writing 4, page 23

A (10 minutes)

1. Direct students to read the sentences and complete the activity. Then have them compare answers with a partner.
2. Elicit the answers from volunteers. You may want to project the page to show the answers.

Grammar A Answers, p. 23

1. Not every (character) that has superpowers is necessarily a superhero.
2. Some superheroes possess (abilities) which they have developed to a superhuman level.
3. At 19, Yohannes Gebregeorgis borrowed (a novel) that changed his life forever.
4. His father was (an illiterate cattle merchant) who insisted that his son have an education.
5. He reads storybooks to (children) who have no access to television.
6. Salva started (a youth environmental group) which is trying to clean up the city.
7. (The trash) Salva's group collects is carried away by llamas.

B (10 minutes)

1. Review the example with the class.
2. Have students combine each pair of sentences. Elicit sentences from volunteers and write them on the board.

Grammar B Answers, p. 23

1. We all aspire to do something that/which other people will respect.
2. Superheroes help people who/that cannot help themselves.
3. Superheroes engage in activities that/which we would like to experience.
4. To me, a person who/that inspires others to do good deeds is a hero.
5. Reading books for pleasure gives students something that/which they cannot get in regular textbooks
6. Caring for the environment is something that/which we can all do.
7. Someone who/that donates money to charity is a generous person.

MULTILEVEL OPTION

Place students in mixed-ability pairs. Higher-level students can help lower-level students complete the activity and explain their understanding.

C (5 minutes)

1. Direct students to read the directions and complete the activity.
2. Elicit answers from volunteers. Ask students to give reasons for their answers based on the discussion of the grammar point on p. 22.

Grammar C Answers, p. 23

You can omit the relative pronouns in sentences 1, 3, 5, and 6.

For additional practice with restrictive relative clauses, have students visit *Q Online Practice.*

Reading and Writing 4, page 24

Unit Assignment:
Write an analysis paragraph

Unit Question (5 minutes)

Refer students back to the ideas they discussed at the beginning of the unit about what makes someone a hero. Cue students if necessary by asking specific questions about the content of the unit: *Who are some superheroes we learned about? What are some qualities that real-life heroes have? How are heroes different from ordinary people?*

Learning Outcome

1. Tie the Unit Assignment to the unit Learning Outcome. Say: *The outcome for this unit is to analyze the qualities that make a person a hero and give examples of the accomplishments of heroes. This Unit Assignment is going to let you show your skill in writing a well-structured paragraph with restrictive relative clauses.*
2. Explain that you are going to use a rubric similar to their Self-Assessment checklist on p. 26 to grade their Unit Assignment. You can also share a copy of the Unit Assignment Rubric (on p. 12 of this *Teacher's Handbook*) with the students.

Plan and Write

Brainstorm

A (15 minutes)

1. Have a volunteer read the directions aloud. Remind students to use information from both readings to support their ideas.
2. Direct students to fill in the chart with ideas for their essays. Monitor and provide feedback.
3. Then have students compare the people, qualities, and accomplishments in their chart.

Reading and Writing 4, page 25

Plan

B (20 minutes)

1. Review the parts of a paragraph: a topic sentence with a controlling idea, supporting sentences, and a concluding sentence.
2. Direct students to complete their outlines.
3. Monitor and provide help as needed.

Write

C (20 minutes)

1. Go over the Self-Assessment checklist on p. 26 with students before they begin writing. Remind them that you will be using a similar rubric to evaluate their writing.
2. Read the directions aloud. Point out the transition word in the box. Direct students to write their analysis paragraphs. Remind them that this is their opportunity to combine the skills and information they have learned throughout the whole unit.

Alternative Unit Assignments

Assign or have students choose one of these assignments to do instead of, or in addition to, the Unit Assignment.

1. Write a comparison of a superhero and an everyday hero.
2. Write a superhero story.

For an additional unit assignment, have students visit *Q Online Practice.*

▶ *Reading and Writing 4, page 26*

Revise and Edit

Peer Review

A (15 minutes)

1. Pair students and direct them to read each other's work
2. Ask students to answer and discuss the questions.
3. Give students suggestions of helpful feedback: *I think you could describe this quality more. Maybe you should give an example here.*

Rewrite

B (10 minutes)

Students should review their partners' answers from A and rewrite their paragraphs if necessary.

Edit

C (10 minutes)

1. Direct students to read and complete the Self-Assessment checklist. They should be prepared to hand in their work or discuss it in class.
2. Ask for a show of hands for how many students gave all or mostly *yes* answers.
3. Use the Unit Assignment Rubric on p. 12 in this *Teacher's Handbook* to score each student's assignment.
4. Alternatively, divide the class into large groups and have students read their paragraphs to their group. Pass out copies of the Unit Assignment Rubric and have students grade each other.

▶ *Reading and Writing 4, page 27*

Track Your Success (5 minutes)

1. Have students circle the words they have learned in this unit. Suggest that students go back through the unit to review any words they have forgotten.
2. Have students check the skills they have mastered. If students need more practice to feel confident about their proficiency in a skill, point out the page numbers and encourage them to review.
3. Read the Learning Outcome aloud. Ask students if they feel that they have met the outcome.

Unit Assignment Rubric

Student name: ____

Date: __________

Unit Assignment: *Write an analysis paragraph.*

20 points = Paragraph element was completely successful (at least 90% of the time).
15 points = Paragraph element was mostly successful (at least 70% of the time).
10 points = Paragraph element was partially successful (at least 50% of the time).
0 points = Paragraph element was not successful.

Write an Analysis Paragraph	20 points	15 points	10 points	0 points
Paragraph describes the qualities of a hero.				
Paragraph includes a clear topic sentence with at least three supporting details.				
Restrictive relative clauses are used correctly.				
Appropriate transition words are used correctly (if included).				
Punctuation, spelling, and grammar are correct.				

Total points: __________

Comments:

UNIT 2

Unit QUESTION
What makes you want to buy something?

Appearances

READING • annotating and highlighting a text
VOCABULARY • collocations with nouns
WRITING • writing a descriptive essay
GRAMMAR • definite and indefinite articles

LEARNING OUTCOME

Describe aspects of a product or service to make someone want to purchase or use it.

Reading and Writing 4, pages 28–29

Preview the Unit

Learning Outcome

1. Ask for a volunteer to read the unit skills and the unit Learning Outcome.
2. Explain: *This is what you are expected to be able to do by the unit's end. The Learning Outcome explains how you are going to be evaluated. With this outcome in mind, you should focus on learning those skills (Reading, Vocabulary, Writing, Grammar) that will support your goal of describing a product or service to make people want to buy or use it. You can also act as a mentor in the classroom to help your classmates learn the skills and meet this Learning Outcome.*

A (15 minutes)

1. Elicit students' opinions about shopping. Ask: *When was the last time you went shopping? Where did you go? Do you like shopping?*
2. Put students in pairs or small groups to discuss the first two questions.
3. Call on volunteers to share their ideas with the class. Ask: *What makes shopping fun (or not fun)? What was the last thing that you bought that you didn't need? What made you buy it?*
4. Focus students' attention on the photo. Have a volunteer describe the photo to the class. Read the third question aloud. Elicit students' answers.

Preview the Unit A Answers, p. 29
Answers will vary. Sample answers:
1. I like to shop for clothes. / I don't enjoy shopping for electronics.
2. I buy things based on how they look. For example, I don't buy clothes in colors that I don't like.
3. Yes, I would want to shop in a market like this. The prices are better in these markets than in big stores.

B (15 minutes)

1. Introduce the Unit Question: "What makes you want to buy something?" Ask related information questions or questions about personal experience to help students prepare for answering the more abstract Unit Question. *Think of stores that you shop in. What does the store do to make their products look good and sell them? What items are in the store windows?*
2. Put students into small groups and give each group a piece of poster paper and a marker.
3. Read the Unit Question aloud. Give students a minute to silently consider their answers to the question. Tell students to pass the paper and the marker around the group. Direct each group member to write a different answer to the question. Encourage them to help one another.
4. Ask each group to choose a reporter to read the answers to the class. Point out similarities and differences among the answers. If answers from different groups are similar, make a group list that incorporates the answers. Post the list to refer to later in the unit.

Preview the Unit B Answers, p. 29
Answers will vary. Sample answers:
Lower-level answer: I like to buy things that have a low price.
On-level answer: I like to buy brands that are popular and good quality.
Higher-level answer: Usually, I like to buy things that look good and that make me feel good about spending my money.

The Q Classroom (5 minutes)

CD1, Track 5

1. Play *The Q Classroom*. Use the example from the audio to help students continue the conversation. Ask: How did the students answer the question? Do you agree or disagree with their ideas? Why?
2. Have students compare the reasons students gave in the audio to their lists from Activity B. They should add any new ideas from the listening.

Reading and Writing 4, page 30

C (10 minutes)

1. Preview the questionnaire.
2. Direct students to complete the questionnaire and then share their answers with a partner.

MULTILEVEL OPTION

Pair lower-level students and have them work together to complete the activity.

When higher-level students have finished, ask them to write two additional questions for the questionnaire. Discuss these questions and possible answers as a class.

Preview the Unit C Answers, p. 30

Answers will vary.

D (10 minutes)

1. Have partners discuss the questions.
2. Survey the class to see if one of the descriptions was chosen more than the others.

Preview the Unit D Answers, p. 30

Answers will vary. Sample answers:

1. I'm a convenient shopper. I always go shopping when there's a sale . My partner is a practical shopper. She always goes shopping with a list and buys only the things she needs.
2. I'm a convenient shopper most of the time but I can sometimes be a trendy shopper. I like to buy brand names when they're on sale.

EXPANSION ACTIVITY: Survey Your Classmates (15 minutes)

1. Before surveying the class, have students survey each other. Students should ask each other about the type of shopper they are and share related personal experiences or anecdotes.
2. Ask students to survey at least five students and note their answers. Discuss the results as a class.

READING

Reading and Writing 4, page 31

READING 1: So Much Dead Space

VOCABULARY (15 minutes)

1. Ask students to read each sentence, try to guess the meaning of the bold word, and then circle the correct definition.
2. Have partners compare answers. Then elicit the answers from volunteers. Discuss the context clues that helped them choose the correct definitions.
3. Pronounce each word and have students repeat.

Vocabulary Answers, pp. 31-32

1. a;	**2.** a;	**3.** b;	**4.** a;
5. b;	**6.** a;	**7.** b;	**8.** a;
9. a;	**10.** a;	**11.** b	

For additional practice with the vocabulary, have students visit *Q Online Practice*.

Reading and Writing 4, page 32

PREVIEW READING 1 (5 minutes)

1. Ask a volunteer to read the introduction aloud. Place students into pairs to discuss their answers.
2. Tell students they should review their answers after reading.

Preview Reading 1 Answers, p. 32

Answers will vary. Sample answers:

I usually see clothes and shoes in store windows.

Yes, I have. Yesterday I saw a great pair of a shoes in a window and I went into the store to see how much they cost. They were too expensive.

Reading 1 Background Note

The job of a window display designer is one that most people have probably never thought about. The designer doesn't just put clothes on mannequins and place them in the store windows. The designer must analyze what is popular and display the items in a way that gets people to go inside the store. In the past, window displays served the function of showing the sheer number and variety of products you could buy in a store. Today, however, window displays are often more artistic than functional. The designer may even attempt to send a social or political message through his or her displays.

READ (20 minutes)

CD1, Track 6

1. Instruct students to read the article. Remind them to refer to the glossed words as they read.
2. When students have finished reading, answer any questions about the article or additional vocabulary.
3. Play the audio and have students follow along.

Reading and Writing 4, page 34

MAIN IDEAS (10 minutes)

1. Have students complete the activity individually.
2. Then have partners compare answers. Remind students to go back to the article to find information to support their answers.
3. Elicit the answers from volunteers.

Main Ideas Answers, pp. 34-35

1. c; **2.** a; **3.** c; **4.** b; **5.** c

Reading and Writing 4, page 35

DETAILS (15 minutes)

1. Direct students to answer the questions and then compare their answers with a partner.
2. Go over the answers as the class. Help students understand what "quick read" means in number 5.

Details Answers, p. 35

1. Last century, pedestrians strolled and took time to look in store windows. Now most people walk fast and look straight ahead.

2. A "pile" of people forms and stays crowded together after they cross. Behind them is a gap of fewer people.

3. They are crowded with many products, so it's difficult to focus on any product clearly.

4. People read in groups of words, not letter by letter. Movies show the story of a lifetime in just a few hours. A commercial can tell a full story.

5. Store windows must be simple so that shoppers can easily identify the product, and they must be creative to catch someone's eye.

6. Windows that tell jokes. Some are related to history. Some make him laugh.

For additional practice with reading comprehension, have students visit *Q Online Practice.*

Critical Thinking Tip (2 minutes)

1. Ask a volunteer to read the tip aloud.
2. Ask students: *What do you have to do before you can discuss your answers with others?* Answers may include: clarify my understanding of the question, summarize my thoughts, remember what we've discussed about the topic, etc.

Reading and Writing 4, page 36

WHAT DO YOU THINK? (20 minutes)

1. Ask students to read the questions and reflect on their answers.
2. Seat students in small groups and assign roles: a group leader to make sure everyone contributes, a note-taker to record the group's ideas, a reporter to share the group's ideas with the class, and a timekeeper to watch the clock.
3. Give students five minutes to discuss the questions. Call time if conversations are winding down. Allow them an extra minute or two if necessary.
4. Call on each group's reporter to share ideas with the class.
5. Have each student choose one of the questions and write for 5–10 minutes in response.
6. Call on volunteers to share their responses.

MULTILEVEL OPTION:

Have lower-level students work together and choose the same question to respond to.

Ask higher-level students to respond to more than one question.

What Do You Think? Activity Answers, p. 36

Answers will vary. Sample answers:

1. One of my favorite stores is a clothing store. It usually has mannequins in the window wearing the newest clothing. I think their windows are appealing because they're simple.

2. Store owners attract customers by the way they display items inside the store. Also, they may choose lighting and music that are pleasant.

3. Shopping online is different because we are in the comfort of our own homes. We are usually not in a hurry, so stores don't need to capture our attention as quickly. Also, it's easier to look at items because you don't have to look on a crowded rack.

Learning Outcome

Use the Learning Outcome to frame the purpose and relevance of Reading 1. Ask: *What did you learn from Reading 1 that prepares you to describe a product or service that will make someone want to purchase or use it?* (Students learned what makes a good window display. They may want to use some of these ideas when they write their descriptive essays.)

Reading Skill: Annotating and highlighting (20 minutes)

1. Write *annotate* and *highlight* on the board. Ask: *Have you seen these words before? Why would you want to annotate or highlight information?*
2. Read the first paragraph aloud.
3. Place students into small groups and assign groups to be either "annotate" or "highlight." Tell each group that they will have to teach their skill to another group.
4. Have groups read the appropriate section for their skill and discuss it. Create larger groups—pairing "annotate" and "highlight" groups. Ask students to teach each other about the skills.
5. Check comprehension: *What is the purpose of highlighting and annotating? How is annotating different than highlighting? What information should you highlight in a text? What abbreviations can you use when annotating?*

21ST CENTURY SKILLS

Being able to identify key information or ideas in a text will help students be more efficient employees and save them from having to reread a text again. At work, students may need to highlight key points in an email they are sending or in an email they have received. They may also need to annotate their notes from a meeting or presentation. Similarly, they may want to highlight important information in an employment manual or policy document. Encourage students to highlight and annotate a wide range of texts, such as news stories, academic articles, and emails.

Reading and Writing 4, page 37

A (10 minutes)

1. Direct students to read the paragraph and complete the activity individually. Then have them compare answers with a partner.
2. Check the answers as a class.

Reading Skill A Answers, p. 37

Answers will vary, but should include these ideas:

1. the main idea of the paragraph
2. examples (that show how we process information faster)
3. to give a summary and a reason

Tip for Success (2 minutes)

1. Ask a volunteer to read the tip aloud.
2. Ask: *What is the advantage of writing your notes in your notebook?*

B (15 minutes)

1. Have students read the paragraph and complete the task individually. Then have them compare their highlighting and annotations with a partner.
2. You may want to project the paragraph to show the highlighting and annotations. Discuss any variations students may have in their own marks.

Reading Skill B Answers, p. 37

Answers may include the following:

Annotations: S=what makes a good window, EX= Kiehl's shows social issues

Store windows today must be quick reads. They must be simple enough so that the products can be clearly identified, and they must be creative enough to catch the busy pedestrian's eye. Just a brief look at a store window should answer many questions for savvy shoppers: Who is the core market of the store? Does the store fit their personal style or not? How long will a typical trip into the store take? Especially since today's retail market is so competitive, if done right, windows can function as an important brand-identity tool. As retailers, you must know who your customers are, and you must create windows that they will understand. For instance, Kiehl's, which sells all-natural bath and body products, uses its windows as a place for highlighting social issues, which fits with the priorities of its customers.

web For additional practice with annotating and highlighting, have students visit *Q Online Practice.*

▶ *Reading and Writing 4, page 38*

READING 2:
Now On Stage: Your Home!

VOCABULARY (15 minutes)

1. Have students read the words and the definitions. Answer any questions about meaning or provide examples of the words in context.
2. Direct students to fill in the blanks with the bold vocabulary words.
3. Elicit the answers from volunteers. Pronounce each word and have students repeat.

Vocabulary Answers, pp. 38–39

1. visualize;
2. neutral;
3. remove;
4. negative;
5. residence;
6. tend;
7. minimize;
8. potential;
9. feature;
10. mentally;
11. investment;
12. In theory

MULTILEVEL OPTION

Group lower-level students and provide alternate example sentences to help them understand the words. For example, *Doing exercise helps **minimize** stress. They **removed** the car from the garage. Before they sold the house, they painted the walls a **neutral** color.*

Pair higher-level students and have them write an additional sentence for each word. Call on students to write their sentences on the board. Correct the sentences, focusing on the use of the vocabulary rather than other grammatical issues.

For additional practice with the vocabulary, have students visit *Q Online Practice*.

▶ *Reading and Writing 4, page 39*

PREVIEW READING 2 (5 minutes)

Read the introduction. Direct students to look at the photos and discuss the questions in pairs. Elicit answers from volunteers.

Preview Reading 2 Answers, p. 39

Answers will vary. Sample answers:

1. The photos show the same room. In the first photo, the room is messy and there are things all over the floor. In the second photo, the room is clean and some things have been moved.
2. I like the second room because you can see everything.

Reading 2 Background Note

Before sellers decide whether or not to stage their home, they may want to weigh the advantages and disadvantages. Perhaps the most important advantage of staging a home is that the home is likely to sell much faster when it's staged. Another benefit is that staging usually allows the seller to increase the sale price. A disadvantage of staging is that family photos, sentimental items, or things that are used every day may need to be temporarily removed. Of course, the expense of staging may be the biggest disadvantage, though sellers should compare this with the potential benefits before making a decision.

▶ *Reading and Writing 4, page 40*

READ (20 minutes)

CD1, Track 7

1. Instruct students to read the article. Remind them to refer to the glossed words as they read.
2. When students have finished reading, answer any questions they may have about the article or additional vocabulary.
3. Play the audio and have students follow along.

▶ *Reading and Writing 4, page 42*

MAIN IDEAS (10 minutes)

1. Read the directions. Give students a few minutes to do the activity.
2. Call on volunteers to share their answers.

Main Ideas Answers, pp. 42–43

1. a; **2.** b; **3.** b; **4.** a; **5.** c; **6.** a

Reading and Writing 4, page 43

DETAILS (15 minutes)

1. Direct students to complete the chart.
2. Have students compare answers with a partner. Remind them to look back at the article to check their answers.
3. Go over the answers with the class.

Details Answers, p. 43

1. Will make a place look larger.
2. Feature only a few pieces of furniture and pull the pieces away from the walls.
3. Open the drapes or remove them completely.
4. Reduces clutter and helps buyers imagine themselves in the home.
5. Makes rooms appear spacious and neat.
6. Dark colors can make a room seem smaller.
7. Helps buyers imagine an empty space as a home and keeps buyers from seeing the negatives.

web For additional practice with reading comprehension, have students visit *Q Online Practice.*

Reading and Writing 4, page 44

WHAT DO YOU THINK?

A (15 minutes)

1. Ask students to read the questions and reflect on their answers.
2. Seat students in small groups and assign roles: a group leader to make sure everyone contributes, a note-taker to record the group's ideas, a reporter to share the group's ideas with the class, and, a timekeeper to watch the clock.
3. Give students five minutes to discuss the questions. Call time if conversations are winding down. Allow an extra minute or two if necessary.
4. Have students choose one question and write a paragraph in response.
5. Ask volunteers to share their responses.

What Do You Think? Activity A Answers, p. 44

Answers will vary. Sample answers:

1. I would need to remove some of my furniture to make the room look bigger. Also, I would probably add fresh paint to the walls to make the room look new and clean.
2. I think a stager's job is interesting, but I would not be good at it. I don't think I have "an eye" for that sort of work. I often don't pay attention to small details.

B (10 minutes)

1. Tell the students that they should think about both Reading 1 and Reading 2 as they answer the questions in Activity B.
2. Elicit answers from each group's reporter.

What Do You Think? Activity B Answers, p. 44

Answers will vary. Sample answers:

1. The "story" that homeowners want to tell is that they are happy and comfortable in their home. The story should make buyers feel like the home is exactly what they are looking for.
2. Window designers could follow the advice of not making a space look too crowded. Also, they could use bright colors because that makes people happy.

Critical Q: Expansion Activity

Identify Discussion Techniques

Ask: *What are the benefits of discussing your ideas with others?* Review the Critical Thinking Tip on p. 36. Have students reflect on the process of preparing for a discussion. Ask: *What did you think about when you read the questions in Activity B on p. 44? What did you do to prepare for the group discussion?*

Write some of the students' responses on the board. These may include: *I clarified the question with a classmate; I reread a part of the article; I looked up a vocabulary word;* or *I made notes of my answers.*

Learning Outcome

Use the Learning Outcome to frame the purpose and relevance of Readings 1 and 2. Ask: *What did you learn from Readings 1 and 2 that prepares you to describe a product or service that will make someone want to purchase or use it?* (Students learned how window displays can attract shoppers and how home staging can attract homebuyers. They may want to use these ideas when they write their descriptive essays.)

Vocabulary Skill: Collocations with nouns (10 minutes)

1. Ask a volunteer to read the first paragraph. Go over the examples of adjective, verb, and preposition + noun collocations.
2. Check comprehension: What are collocations? Can you think of any other examples of collocations with nouns? Elicit additional examples and categorize them on the board.

Skill Note

The *Oxford Collocations Dictionary for Students of English* includes a wealth of information about words and their collocations. As there are no rules to teach students to help them remember collocations, it's important that they learn to recognize patterns. As you work through each unit, guide students' exploration of collocations by assigning nouns from the vocabulary. Students should look up each noun and list its common collocations, making note of which ones are adjectives, verbs, and prepositions.

Some collocations with nouns from this unit include:

concept: *basic concept; develop a concept; the concept of*

investment: *foreign investment; make an investment; as an investment*

priority: *high priority; take priority over*

▶ ***Reading and Writing 4, page 45***

A (10 minutes)

1. Do number 1 together as a class.
2. Have students complete the activity with a partner.
3. Have volunteers read the sentences aloud.

Vocabulary Skill A Answers, p. 45

1. Social;	**2.** old;
3. modern;	**4.** grab;
5. at;	**6.** full;
7. caught;	**8.** take;
9. quick;	**10.** on;
11. create;	**12.** Over;
13. personal;	**14.** in;
15. give;	**16.** in

Tip for Success (1 minute)

1. Ask a volunteer to read the tip aloud.
2. Explain: *Idioms are challenging because you often cannot look up individual words in the dictionary in order to understand the meaning. A good learner's dictionary will indicate when a collocation is an idiom.*

B (10 minutes)

1. Direct students to write their sentences and then share them with a partner.
2. Ask volunteers to write their sentences on the board. Correct the collocations as a class.

Vocabulary Skill B Answers, p. 45

Answers will vary. Sample answers:

1. I try to focus on one subject *at a time* when I'm doing my homework.
2. I *take pleasure* in setting a good example for my little sister.
3. When I'm window shopping, I only need to take *a quick look* to know if I want to go inside a store.
4. I need the teacher to explain the answer *in a way* that I can understand clearly.
5. His suit *gives me the impression* that he's a businessman.

For additional practice with collocations with nouns, have students visit *Q Online Practice*.

▶ ***Reading and Writing 4, page 46***

WRITING

Writing Skill: Writing a descriptive essay (20 minutes)

1. Read the first paragraph. Then ask volunteers to read the information about the organization and language used in a descriptive essay.
2. Check comprehension: *What does a descriptive essay do? How is it organized? How are the sentences with non-descriptive and descriptive language different? Which type of sentence helps you create a picture in your mind?*

▶ ***Reading and Writing 4, page 47***

A (15 minutes)

1. Direct students to read the essay and complete the activity. Then have them compare answers with a partner.
2. Elicit answers from the class. For number 2, you may want to list students' answers in a chart on the board with each sense as a column head.
3. Explain *head over* in the last paragraph.

Writing Skill A Answers, p. 47

1. Thesis Statement: One of my favorite restaurants is Ben's Diner on Fourth Street because it's perfect for a casual, delicious meal.
   Concluding Sentence: So, whether you're a local, just passing through, or looking for somewhere new to get some great food, I suggest you head over to Ben's.
2. a. sight: gleaming tables, sparkling clean floors, bright green lettuce leaves, deep red tomatoes, purple olives
   b. sound: pleasant noise of conversation, soothing clatter of dishes, sizzling skillet
   c. taste: burger is peppery inside, sharp cheddar cheese, tangy (purple) olives
   d. smell: rich smell of their homemade chicken soup, spicy aroma from the chicken fajitas
   e. touch: soft red leather booths, smooth marble counter, soft toasted bun, burger is crunchy on the outside, moist on the inside

Reading and Writing 4, page 48

B (15 minutes)

1. Discuss the first example. Ask: *What was added to the sentence to make it more descriptive?*
2. Direct students to rewrite the sentences. Ask volunteers to write their sentences on the board.

Writing Skill B Answers, p. 48

Answers will vary. Sample answers:

2. The small room was filled with pink roses, yellow and white daisies, and sweet-smelling purple lilacs.
3. The moist chicken and creamy potatoes were delicious.
4. We went on a long hike through the pine forest.
5. His aunt quietly entered the room on her tiptoes.
6. I couldn't believe that I didn't get to watch the final World Cup match on my friend's new flat-screen TV.

web For additional practice with writing a descriptive essay, have students visit *Q Online Practice.*

Grammar: Definite and indefinite articles (20 minutes)

1. Read the information about articles together.
2. Check comprehension: *When do we use indefinite articles? If the noun is unknown or unimportant to the reader, which kind of article should you use? When do we use definite articles? If the noun relates to something else you have introduced, which kind of article should you use?*

Skill Note

Many students have first languages that do not use articles (Russian, Japanese, etc.), so learning to use articles correctly can be a great challenge. In order to have success with nouns, students must understand the difference between count and non-count nouns. Generally, count nouns are things that can be counted, such as desks, chairs, walls, books, etc. Non-count nouns are usually certain categories of nouns, such as materials (wood, cotton, plastic) and foods (rice, meat, milk, water). Other categories include: sports, languages, fields of study, and natural events. You may want to review count and non-count nouns before discussing articles.

Reading and Writing 4, page 49

Tip for Success (1 minute)

1. Ask a volunteer to read the tip aloud.
2. Point to something in the classroom and ask: *What's this/that?* (your pencil, a book, etc.) *What are these/those?* (some pencils, my shoes, etc.)

A (15 minutes)

1. Direct students to complete each blank in the email with the correct article or no article.
2. Ask volunteers to read the email. Discuss the rules behind the use of some of the articles.

Grammar A Answers, pp. 49–50

1. no article;
2. the;
3. the;
4. a;
5. The;
6. the;
7. the;
8. the;
9. an;
10. the;
11. the;
12. a;
13. the;
14. the;
15. no article;
16. no article;
17. no article;
18. the;
19. a

web For additional practice with definite and indefinite articles, have students visit *Q Online Practice.*

Reading and Writing 4, page 50

Unit Assignment: Write a descriptive essay

Unit Question (5 minutes)

Refer students to the ideas they discussed at the beginning of the unit about what makes them want to buy something. Cue students if necessary by asking specific questions about the unit: *What makes a good window display? How can a window attract shoppers? How does staging a home help sellers and homebuyers?*

Learning Outcome

1. Tie the Unit Assignment to the unit Learning Outcome. Say: *The outcome for this unit is to describe aspects of a product or service to make someone want to purchase or use it. This Unit Assignment is going to let you show your skill in writing a descriptive essay and in using articles and nouns with collocations.*
2. Explain that you are going to use a rubric similar to their Self-Assessment checklist on p. 52 to grade their Unit Assignment. You can also share a copy of the Unit Assignment Rubric (on p. 23 of this Teacher's Handbook) with the students.

Plan and Write

Brainstorm

A (15 minutes)

1. Direct students to complete the task individually.
2. Have them discuss their ideas with a partner to get feedback and choose their product or service.

Reading and Writing 4, page 51

Plan

B (20 minutes)

1. Review the information about essay organization and descriptive language on page 46.
2. Have students use their ideas to complete the outline for their descriptive essay.

Reading and Writing 4, page 52

Write

C (20 minutes)

1. Go over the Self-Assessment checklist on page 52 with students. Remind them that you are going to use a similar rubric to evaluate their writing.
2. Direct students to use the information in their outlines to create paragraphs for their essays. Remind them to use descriptive language.

Alternative Unit Assignments

Assign or have students choose one of these assignments to do instead of, or in addition to, the Unit Assignment.

1. Write an essay describing an advertisement, store window, or Web page you've seen. State who the intended customer is, how the advertisement, window, or Web page tries to attract customers, and whether or not it is effective.
2. Write a paragraph describing a room that you like. Include information about light, color, furniture placement, shape, and overall feel.

For an additional Unit Assignment, have students visit *Q Online Practice.*

Revise and Edit

Peer Review

A (15 minutes)

1. Pair students and direct them to read each other's work.
2. Ask students to answer and discuss the questions.
3. Give students suggestions of helpful feedback: *Can you describe this a little more? There was a problem with articles in the last paragraph.*

Rewrite

B (10 minutes)

Students should review their partners' answers from A and rewrite their paragraphs if necessary.

Edit

C (10 minutes)

1. Direct students to read and complete the Self-Assessment checklist. They should be prepared to hand in their work or discuss it in class.
2. Ask for a show of hands for how many students gave all or mostly yes answers.
3. Use the Unit Assignment Rubric on p. 23 in this *Teacher's Handbook* to score each student's assignment.
4. Alternatively, divide the class into large groups and have students read their paragraphs to their group. Pass out copies of the Unit Assignment Rubric and have students grade each other.

Reading and Writing 4, page 53

Track Your Success (5 minutes)

1. Have students circle the words they have learned in this unit. Suggest that students go back through the unit to review any words they have forgotten.
2. Have students check the skills they have mastered. If students need more practice to feel confident about their proficiency in a skill, point out the page numbers and encourage them to review.
3. Read the Learning Outcome aloud. Ask students if they feel that they have met the outcome.

Unit Assignment Rubric

Student name: ____

Date: ___________

Unit Assignment: *Write a descriptive essay.*

20 points = Essay element was completely successful (at least 90% of the time).
15 points = Essay element was mostly successful (at least 70% of the time).
10 points = Essay element was partially successful (at least 50% of the time).
0 points = Essay element was not successful.

Write a Descriptive Essay	20 points	15 points	10 points	0 points
Essay clearly describes the product, business, or service.				
Introduction catches the reader's interest and expresses a clear opinion.				
Each body paragraph includes a topic sentence and descriptive language.				
Articles are used correctly.				
Collocations with nouns are used correctly.				

Total points: ___________

Comments:

UNIT 3

Unit QUESTION

What important lessons do we learn as children?

Growing Up

READING • making inferences
VOCABULARY • prefixes and suffixes
WRITING • organizing a narrative
GRAMMAR • past perfect

LEARNING OUTCOME

Relate a personal memory of someone or something that influenced you when you were younger.

Reading and Writing 4, pages 54–55

Preview the Unit

Learning Outcome

1. Ask for a volunteer to read the unit skills and the unit Learning Outcome.
2. Explain: *This is what you are expected to be able to do by the unit's end. The Learning Outcome explains how you are going to be evaluated. With this outcome in mind, you should focus on learning those skills (Reading, Vocabulary, Writing, Grammar) that will support your goal of relating a personal memory from when you were younger. You can also act as a mentor in the classroom to help your classmates learn the skills and meet this Learning Outcome.*

A (15 minutes)

1. Ask students: *What comes to mind when you think about "growing up?" Is "growing up" easy or hard?*
2. Put students in pairs or small groups to discuss the first two questions.
3. Call on volunteers to share their ideas with the class. Ask: *Did you and your partner have a similar childhood? Did you disagree with your parents when you were a child?*
4. Focus students' attention on the photo. Have a volunteer describe the photo to the class. Read the third question aloud. Elicit students' answers.

Preview the Unit A Answers, p. 55

Answers will vary. Sample answers:

1. I remember my first day of school. I was scared and excited at the same time.
2. Parents and their children sometimes disagree about what the child eats or wears.
3. I think the child feels nervous about being punished. I think the mother is angry with the boy.

B (15 minutes)

1. Introduce the Unit Question: "What important lessons do we learn as children?" Ask related information questions or questions about personal experience to help students prepare for answering the more abstract Unit Question. For example, ask: *Did your parents teach you to say "please" and "thank you"? What things did your parents or other family members teach you? Do you (Would you) teach the same things to your children?*
2. Read the Unit Question aloud. Tell the students: *Let's start off our discussion by listing lessons we learned as children.*
3. Seat students in small groups and direct them to pass around a paper as quickly as they can, with each group member adding one item to the list. Tell them they have 2 minutes to make the lists, and they should write as much as possible.
4. Call time and ask a reporter from each group to read the list aloud.
5. Use items from the list as a springboard for discussion. For example, say: *Let's talk about "how to get along with others." What do you remember about learning this lesson as a child?*

Preview the Unit B Answers, p. 55

Answers will vary. Sample answers:
Lower-level answer: We learn important lessons from our parents. We learn how to be a good person.
On-level answer: One important lesson we learn from our parents is how to be a good person. This may include being polite, helping others, and obeying the rules.
Higher-level answer: As children we learn many important lessons from our parents, such as how to be polite, help others, and, of course, obey the rules.

The Q Classroom (5 minutes)

CD1, Track 8

1. Play *The Q Classroom*. Use the example from the audio to help students continue the conversation. Ask: *How did the students answer the question? Do you agree or disagree with their ideas? Why?*
2. Ask students to look over the answers they wrote for Activity B. Elicit and add any ideas from the audio that aren't already included.

Reading and Writing 4, page 56

C (15 minutes)

1. For the survey, pair up students who may not know each other very well. Remind students to write short answers in the survey instead of complete sentences.
2. When students have finished, call on volunteers to share information about their partner.

MULTILEVEL OPTION

Pair lower-level students and give them time to read the questions before interviewing each other. This will give them a chance to think about their own answers. Answer any questions they may have about unfamiliar vocabulary.

Higher-level students may start interviewing each other immediately, which will give them more time for the discussion in Activity D.

Preview the Unit C Answers, p. 56

Answers will vary.

D (10 minutes)

1. As students finish Activity C, tell them to read the directions and answer the questions.
2. Elicit answers from volunteers.

Preview the Unit D Answers, p. 56

Answers will vary. Sample answers:

1. My partner's behavior has changed the most since he was a child. When he was young, he was really active and always got into trouble at school. Now he's very quiet and hard-working.
2. A lot has changed for my partner since he was a child. He used to live in a big house in a small town. Now he lives in a small apartment in a big city. He had a dog when he was a child. Now he has a cat.

EXPANSION ACTIVITY:
Compare and Contrast (10 minutes)

1. Choose a question from the survey that shows how students have changed over time. (Questions 2, 3, and 5 are well suited for this activity.) Make a T-chart on the board and label each column with one of the questions. For example, the two column headings for Question 3 would be: *What did you want to be when you grew up?* and *What do you want to be now?*
2. Call on volunteers to share their partner's answers (e.g., *Sam wanted to be a doctor. Now he wants to be a lawyer)*. Write the answers in the chart.
3. Ask students to write sentences comparing and contrasting their classmates. For example: *Sam wanted to be a doctor, and so did Anabel.*

READING

Reading and Writing 4, page 57

READING 1: The Good Teen

VOCABULARY (15 minutes)

1. Call on students to read the vocabulary words and definitions aloud. Answer any questions about meaning or provide examples of the words in context. Pronounce each word and have students repeat. Highlight the syllable that receives primary stress in each word.
2. Have students complete each sentence with the correct vocabulary word.
3. Have students compare answers with a partner. Then call on volunteers to read the sentences.

MULTILEVEL OPTION

Group lower-level students and provide alternate example sentences to help them understand the words. For example, *My **colleagues** at work are very helpful. I need to **select** the best person for the job.*

Pair higher-level students and have them write an additional sentence for each word. Have volunteers write their sentences on the board. Correct the sentences, focusing on the use of the vocabulary rather than other grammatical issues.

Vocabulary Answers, pp. 57–58

1. colleague;	**2.** consistent with;
3. theoretically;	**4.** accurately;
5. extracurricular;	**6.** select;
7. equipped with;	**8.** competence;
9. nurture;	**10.** assumption;
11. innate;	**12.** period

web For additional practice with the vocabulary, have students visit *Q Online Practice*.

Reading and Writing 4, page 58

PREVIEW READING 1 (10 minutes)

1. Ask a volunteer to read the introduction aloud. Elicit the ages when a person is a teenager.
2. Direct students to write their ideas and then share them with a partner. Call on students to share their answers with the class.
3. Tell students to review their answers after reading.

Preview Reading 1 Answer, p. 58

Answers will vary but may include beliefs that teenagers are moody or sensitive, have difficulty with their parents, or face a lot of peer pressure from their friends.

Reading 1 Background Note

Dr. Laurence Steinberg, a distinguished university professor at Temple University, believes that teenagers' brains are different from adults' brains. His research has shown that the brain of a young person is still developing, even until the mid-20s. He has found that the part of the brain that controls decision-making and comparing risks with rewards is not yet mature. This may explain why many teenagers take risks that they would never consider as adults, such as driving too fast. Dr. Steinberg plans to expand his research internationally to see if his findings about the adolescent brain are consistent across cultures.

The study by Dr. Richard Lerner that is mentioned in the article is a 4–H study. 4–H is the largest youth development organization in the U.S.

Reading and Writing 4, page 59

READ (20 minutes)

CD1, Track 9

1. Instruct students to read the article. Remind them to refer to the glossed words as they read.
2. When students have finished reading, answer any questions they may have about the article or additional vocabulary.
3. Play the audio and have students follow along.

Critical Q: Expansion Activity

Evaluate Recommendations

Paragraphs 6–9 in Reading 1 give several recommendations about good parenting and what teenagers need. Have students identify the recommendations and decide whether they agree or disagree with them. As students evaluate the recommendations, they should make note of their reasons for their opinions.

Then have students share their opinions with a partner. Have pairs ultimately decide which recommendation is the most important. Finally, have the pairs compare the recommendations from the reading to beliefs about good parenting in their home cultures.

Reading and Writing 4, page 61

MAIN IDEAS (15 minutes)

1. Ask volunteers to share some main ideas that they remember from the article.
2. Have students answer the questions individually. Then elicit answers from volunteers.

Main Ideas Answers, p. 61

1. Adolescence is a difficult period (including poor decisions, hanging out with the wrong friends, taking risks, refusing to follow rules, not talking to parents).
2. The Five C's are competence, confidence, connection, character, and caring.
3. Eliza has the Five Cs.
4. Teens need opportunities that nurture positive interactions with adults, develop life skills, and give them the chance to show leadership.
5. Good parenting nurtures qualities like honesty, empathy, self-reliance, kindness, cooperation, self-control, and cheerfulness.

DETAILS (10 minutes)

1. Direct students to mark the statements *T* or *F*.
2. Have students compare answers with a partner. Remind them to look back at the article to check their answers.
3. Go over the answers with the class. Elicit corrections for any false statements.

Details Answers, p. 61

1. T;	**2.** T;	**3.** F;	**4.** T;
5. F;	**6.** T;	**7.** T;	**8.** F

 For additional practice with reading comprehension, have students visit *Q Online Practice*.

Reading and Writing 4, page 62

WHAT DO YOU THINK? (20 minutes)

1. Ask students to read the questions and reflect on their answers.
2. Seat students in small groups and assign roles: a group leader to make sure everyone contributes, a note-taker to record the group's ideas, a reporter to share the group's ideas with the class, and a timekeeper to watch the clock.
3. Give students five minutes to discuss the questions. Call time if conversations are winding down. Allow them an extra minute or two if necessary.
4. Call on each group's reporter to share ideas with the class.
5. Have each student choose one of the questions and write for 5–10 minutes in response.
6. Call on volunteers to share their responses.

MULTILEVEL OPTION:

Put students in mixed-ability groups to discuss the questions. This way, higher-level students will provide vocabulary or key ideas for their lower-level partners. For the response writing, pair lower-level students and have them choose the same question to respond to.

As higher-level students finish, have them share their response with a partner.

What Do You Think? Activity Answers, p. 62

Answers will vary. Sample answers:

1. Speaking in public involves confidence, because it can be scary, and connection, because you need to communicate with others. / Playing on a sports team requires competence in a physical skill and confidence that you can play. You also have to connect with your teammates. / Reading to children requires competence, because you must be able to read, and connection, and caring, because working with children requires patience.

2. Other activities include doing chores, having a part-time job, and participating in school clubs.

3. I can remember having very little confidence when I was younger. Even when I knew the answer in school, I was too nervous to say it. My teacher helped me to be less scared. She called on me often, and slowly I felt better about sharing my answers.

Critical Thinking Tip (1 minute)

1. Ask for a volunteer to read the tip aloud.
2. Explain: *When you learn new information, it is helpful to relate it to your personal life. If you can connect the Five Cs to your childhood, you will better understand what the Five Cs are.*

Learning Outcome

Use the Learning Outcome to frame the purpose and relevance of Reading 1. Ask: *What did you learn from Reading 1 that prepares you to relate a personal memory of someone or something that influenced you when you were younger?* (Students read about ways teenagers can develop five positive characteristics—the Five Cs. These ideas may help them when they share their own memories.)

Reading Skill: Making inferences (10 minutes)

1. Ask students if they've heard the phrase "Read between the lines." Explain that the phrase means that sometimes the words they read or hear do not tell them everything. They have to look for or discover the meaning in something even when it is not stated directly.
2. Ask a volunteer to read the information about making inferences. Explain to students that when they make inferences, they are reading between the lines.
3. Check comprehension: *What does it mean to make inferences? Why are inferences useful? Can you think of a time recently when you had to make an inference?*

21ST CENTURY SKILLS

Employers in many fields seek workers who can use information to make independent decisions and take action. The ability to make inferences will help students to be more independent in the workplace. At work, students may need to make inferences from emails or discussions with supervisors or colleagues about what action needs to be taken next. Have students brainstorm ways that this skill would be useful in the workplace. You may also want to discuss situations in which students should probably check their inference with a supervisor before taking action.

Reading and Writing 4, page 63

A (15 minutes)

1. Direct students to check the inferences. Have them underline the information in the paragraph that helped them choose each inference.
2. Have partners compare answers.
3. Then elicit answers from volunteers.

Reading Skill A Answers, p. 63

The following items are checked:

1. Eliza likes sports.
3. Eliza speaks well in public.
6. Eliza is a very busy person.
7. Eliza enjoys spending time with her parents.
10. Eliza is a confident person.

Tip for Success (1 minute)

1. Ask a volunteer to read the tip aloud.
2. Explain: *You should not let your opinion influence your interpretation of the author's words. Inferences should be based on what the author says, not your opinion about what he or she says.*
3. Tell students that they should use statements from the author to support their inferences.

B (10 minutes)

1. Read the directions. Direct students to complete the activity individually and then compare answers with a partner.
2. Elicit answers from volunteers. Have students explain their answers based on the information in the paragraph.

Reading Skill B Answers, pp. 63-64

1. a (*When I was a young child…*)
2. a and b (The writer mentions older siblings.)
3. a and b (*I have always had to struggle to get out of bed in the morning; When I was a young child, the problem wasn't so bad*)
4. a (The writer's father would knock on the door at 6:00.)
5. a (The writer would respond, "One or the other, Dad.")

For additional practice with making inferences, have students visit *Q Online Practice.*

Reading and Writing 4, page 64

READING 2: Bird by Bird

VOCABULARY (15 minutes)

1. Have students read the vocabulary words and definitions. Answer any questions about meaning or provide examples of the words in context.
2. Pronounce each bold word and have students repeat. Highlight the syllable that receives primary stress in each word.
3. Direct students to complete each sentence with a vocabulary word.
4. Ask volunteers to read the sentences aloud.

Vocabulary Answers, pp. 64–65

1. motivate; **2.** exaggerate; **3.** rely on;
4. capture; **5.** significance; **6.** episode;
7. refuge; **8.** suspect; **9.** impassioned;
10. profound; **11.** creative; **12.** resentful

For additional practice with the vocabulary, have students visit *Q Online Practice.*

Reading and Writing 4, page 65

PREVIEW READING 2 (10 minutes)

1. Read the introduction aloud. Ask a volunteer to remind the class what skimming means.
2. Tell students they should skim, not read, the excerpt because you will only give them 5 minutes to complete the task.
3. Tell students they should review their answer after reading.

Preview Reading 2 Answer, p. 65

Checked: She decided to become a writer because of her father.

Reading 2 Background Note

Professional artists, including writers, painters, and performers, teach in San Quentin Prison through the Prison Arts Project. The philosophy of this program is that the skills prisoners use in creating art can be transferred to other aspects of their lives outside of prison. Prisoners learn problem-solving, self-discipline, and concentration skills through their participation in artistic projects. Research shows that those involved in the Prison Arts Project have fewer disciplinary problems and are more likely to stay out of prison once they are released.

▶ *Reading and Writing 4, page 66*

READ (20 minutes)

CD1, Track 10

1. Instruct students to read the excerpt. Remind them to refer to the glossed words as they read.
2. When students have finished reading, answer any questions they may have about the excerpt or about additional vocabulary. Point out that the author is being humorous in paragraph 7 when she says, "I think that this sort of person often becomes either a writer or a career criminal."
3. Play the audio and have students follow along.

▶ *Reading and Writing 4, page 68*

MAIN IDEAS (10 minutes)

1. Have students read the main ideas, find them in the excerpt, and number them in order.
2. Have students compare answers with a partner, looking back at the text to resolve discrepancies.
3. Elicit the answers from volunteers.

Main Ideas Answers, p. 68

a. 3; **b.** 2; **c.** 5; **d.** 7; **e.** 1; **f.** 4; **g.** 6

▶ *Reading and Writing 4, page 69*

DETAILS (10 minutes)

1. Direct students to read the sentences and circle the best answer.
2. Have students compare answers with a partner. Remind them to look back at the excerpt to check their answers.
3. Go over the answers. Discuss the details in each sentence that helped them make the correct inference.

Details Answers, p. 69

1. b; **2.** a; **3.** b; **4.** b; **5.** a

web For additional practice with reading comprehension, have students visit Q Online Practice.

WHAT DO YOU THINK?

A (15 minutes)

1. Ask students to read the questions and reflect on their answers.
2. Seat students in small groups and assign roles: a group leader to make sure everyone contributes, a note-taker to record the group's ideas, a reporter to share the group's ideas with the class, and a timekeeper to watch the clock.
3. Give students five minutes to discuss the questions. Call time if conversations are winding down. Allow them an extra minute or two if necessary.
4. Then have students choose one question and write a paragraph in response.
5. Call on volunteers to share their responses.

What Do You Think? Activity A Answers, p. 69

1. I admire my aunt. She is very smart and independent. She has traveled to many interesting places.

2. My father influenced me as a teenager. He always gave me space to have fun, but he also expected me to do well at school and in sports. He helped me become responsible.

▶ *Reading and Writing 4, page 70*

B (10 minutes)

1. Students may want to switch roles for Activity B. Tell them to think about both Reading 1 and Reading 2 as they answer the questions.
2. Call on each group's reporter to share ideas with the class.

What Do You Think? Activity B Answers, p. 70

1. The author of Reading 2 shows competence in writing and telling stories. She is also funny.

2. Her father taught her, by example, to pay attention to, or be connected with, what was happening around her. This helped her when she wanted to tell a story about an event.

Learning Outcome

Use the Learning Outcome to frame the purpose and relevance of Readings 1 and 2. Ask: *What did you learn from Readings 1 and 2 that prepares you to relate a personal memory of someone or something that influenced you when you were younger?* (Students learned how parents influence or teach their children. They may use these ideas when they relate their own memories.)

Vocabulary Skill: Prefixes and suffixes (10 minutes)

1. Ask a volunteer to read the information about prefixes. Ask: *What is a prefix? What are some examples of prefixes?* Elicit other words that begin with the prefixes.
2. Have another volunteer read the information about suffixes. Ask: *What is a suffix? What are some examples of suffixes?* Elicit other words that end with the suffixes.
3. Ask: *How can knowing about prefixes and suffixes help you improve your English?*

Skill Note

Students may know more prefixes and suffixes than they realize. When you come across words with prefixes or suffixes in a reading or listening, show students how to separate the words. For example, the word *invisible* has the prefix *in-* plus the word *visible*. If students know that *in-* means "not," they can guess the meaning of *invisible* as "not visible."

Encourage students to use this technique with new words. They should be able to recognize common prefixes and suffixes and try to guess the meanings of words based on the prefixes and suffixes.

Reading and Writing 4, page 71

A (10 minutes)

1. Direct students to fill in each blank with a prefix.
2. Go over the answers with the class. Discuss the meanings of the words with prefixes.

Vocabulary Skill A Answers, p. 71

1. mis; **2.** extra; **3.** inter; **4.** re;
5. mid; **6.** anti; **7.** co; **8.** in

B (10 minutes)

1. Ask a volunteer to read the directions aloud.
2. Model the first item. Ask: *Which part of speech is recognize?* (verb) Tell students to check the Verb column. Ask: *How did you know it was a verb?* (the suffix *–ize*)

Vocabulary Skill B Answers, p. 70

1. verb; **2.** noun; **3.** adjective;
4. verb; **5.** adjective; **6.** noun;
7. verb; **8.** noun; **9.** adjective;
10. noun; **11.** noun; **12.** adjective

For additional practice with prefixes and suffixes, have students visit *Q Online Practice*.

C (15 minutes)

1. Direct students to write 5 sentences.
2. Ask volunteers to write their sentences on the board. As a class, check that prefixes and suffixes are used correctly.

Vocabulary Skill C Answers, p. 71

Answers will vary. Sample answers:

1. I didn't recognize my friend from childhood.
2. I enjoy peaceful activities like gardening.
3. She made a large contribution to the hospital.
4. I need a map to navigate the city.
5. Playing sports can help children build confidence.

Reading and Writing 4, page 72

WRITING

Writing Skill: Organizing a narrative essay (10 minutes)

1. Ask for volunteers to read aloud the information about the organization of a narrative essay.
2. Check comprehension: *What is a narrative essay? How is it organized? What does the introduction do? How are the body paragraphs organized? What does the conclusion do?*
3. Read the information about expressing the order of events and the examples listed. Check comprehension: *What language can you use to show the order of events?*
4. Elicit any additional examples for each category (prepositions, time expressions, or time clauses).

A (15 minutes)

1. Read the directions aloud. Tell students they may want to read the questions on page 73 first so that they know what to look for as they read.
2. Tell students to read the essay and answer the questions. Have them compare answers with a partner. Then elicit answers from volunteers.

Writing Skill A Answers, p. 73

1. a five-year old child and her mother
2. The action takes place in the kitchen of their home.
3. The action takes place when the girl is five.
4. She learned how important caring is and now tries to care for her children in the same way.

▶ *Reading and Writing 4, page 74*

Tip for Success (1 minute)

1. Read the tip aloud. Explain: *Most people like stories with details and descriptive language because you can picture what's happening in your mind.*
2. Look back at the Writing Skill on p. 46 together to remind students about descriptive language.

B (15 minutes)

1. Ask for a volunteer to read the directions aloud.
2. Direct students to complete the outline by filling in information from the narrative essay.
3. Discuss the outline as a class.

Writing Skill B Answers, p. 74

I. Introductory Ideas: When I think about my mother, the first thing I think of is her collection of china cups and saucers.
II. A. Important or interesting detail: My mother never wanted to let me.
B. Sometimes I begged until she let me take them down and clean them.
III. Body paragraph 2: Main event in story: My earliest memory of washing the cups was when I was five.
B. I filled the sink with soapy water and began to wash the tiny cups.
IV. Body paragraph 3: Main event in story: As I was washing the cups, I broke my favorite cup.
A. Important or interesting detail: My mother only smiled and said we would glue it back together.
V. Conclusion (What I learned): I will always remember that she cared more about encouraging me than about her valuable cups.

For additional practice with organizing a narrative essay, have students visit *Q Online Practice.*

▶ *Reading and Writing 4, page 75*

Grammar: Past perfect (15 minutes)

1. Call on volunteers to read the information about the past perfect and the examples.
2. Have students identify which action in each sentence happened first.
3. Check comprehension: *What does the past perfect show? What are some examples of the past perfect?*

Skill Note

The past perfect is often used to give background information about what was happening before something else occurred. Since *had* is used for all subjects, students should not find it too difficult to form the past perfect. However, it is important to help them recognize when to use it.

Some additional time clauses used with the past perfect are *before* and *after*. For example, *I had eaten breakfast before I went to school.* However, if it is clear that one action occurred before the other, we often use the simple past for both: *I ate breakfast before I went to school.*

▶ *Reading and Writing 4, page 76*

A (10 minutes)

1. Direct students to read the sentences and complete the activity individually.
2. Put students in pairs to discuss their answers.
3. Elicit answer from volunteers.

Grammar A Answers, p. 76

2. I (1) had only washed a few when the beautiful blue and white cup (2) (slipped) from my small hands.
3. I (1) had forgotten to call my brother, so he (2) (was) angry with me.
4. She (1) had thought seriously about studying medicine, but in the end she (2) (decided) to study business.
5. Until he (2) (got) an internship at a big ad agency, he (1) hadn't been interested in working in advertising.
6. I (2) (didn't answer) the man because I (1) hadn't heard him clearly.

B (10 minutes)

1. Direct students to complete the activity in pairs.
2. Have students write the sentences on the board.

Grammar B Answers, p. 76

1. I had offered to pay for lunch when I realized that I didn't have any money.
2. I had not left my home country until I visited Canada.
3. He had already finished reading the book when he went to see the movie.
4. After they had recalled important events from their past, the students wrote stories about their memories of childhood
5. I had had lunch by the time she arrived at the restaurant.

For additional practice with the past perfect, have students visit *Q Online Practice.*

Reading and Writing 4, page 77

Unit Assignment: Write a narrative essay

Unit Question (5 minutes)

Refer students back to the ideas they discussed at the beginning of the unit about important lessons they learned in childhood. Cue students by asking specific questions about the content of the unit: *What are some of your early childhood memories? What lessons do parents teach children? How can parents, family members, or teachers influence children?*

Learning Outcome

1. Tie the Unit Assignment to the unit Learning Outcome. Say: *The outcome for this unit is to write a narrative essay about a memory of someone or something that had an influence on you when you were younger. This Unit Assignment is going to let you show your skill at writing a narrative essay and using prefixes, suffixes, and the past perfect correctly.*
2. Explain that you are going to use a rubric similar to their Self-Assessment checklist on p. 78 to grade their Unit Assignment. You can also share a copy of the Unit Assignment Rubric (on p. 34 of this *Teacher's Handbook*) with the students.

Plan and Write

Brainstorm

A (15 minutes)

1. Direct students to record their own ideas by copying the organization from the example into their notebooks.
2. Students should share their ideas in small groups and ask their classmates questions to generate more ideas for their essays.

Tip for Success (1 minute)

1. Ask for a volunteer to read the tip aloud.
2. Remind students that answering the six *wh-* questions will help them include details in their essay that paints a picture for their readers and makes their writing more interesting.

Plan

B (20 minutes)

1. Tell students to choose one of the people or things and create an outline for their essay, using the outline on p. 74 as a guide.
2. Circulate while the students are writing their outlines to help them generate ideas or direct them back to the example outline on p. 74.

Write

C (20 minutes)

1. Have students look at the Self-Assessment checklist on page 78. Remind them that you will be using a similar rubric to evaluate their writing.
2. Tell students to use their outline to guide them as they write their narrative essays. Remind students to use time words and clauses along with past perfect verbs to practice what they have learned in this unit.

Alternative Unit Assignments

Assign or have students choose one of these assignments to do instead of, or in addition to, the Unit Assignment.

1. Write a narrative about a classmate's memory of something from their childhood or adolescence that influenced who he or she is today. The narrative should have an introduction, a body with at least two paragraphs, and a conclusion.
2. Write a description of yourself as a child.

For an additional Unit Assignment, have students visit *Q Online Practice.*

Reading and Writing 4, page 78

Revise and Edit

Peer Review

A (15 minutes)

1. Pair students and direct them to read each other's work
2. Ask students to answer and discuss the questions.
3. Give students suggestions of helpful feedback: *I like how you described this. You could use a time word here, like when. I think you could put this verb in the past perfect.*

Rewrite

B (10 minutes)

Students should review their partners' answers from A and rewrite their paragraphs if necessary.

Edit

C (10 minutes)

1. Direct students to read and complete the Self-Assessment checklist. They should be prepared to hand in their work or discuss it in class.
2. Ask for a show of hands for how many students gave all or mostly *yes* answers.
3. Use the Unit Assignment Rubric on p. 34 in this *Teacher's Handbook* to score each student's assignment.
4. Alternatively, divide the class into large groups and have students read their paragraphs to their group. Pass out copies of the Unit Assignment Rubric and have students grade each other.

Reading and Writing 4, page 79

Track Your Success (5 minutes)

1. Have students circle the words they have learned in this unit. Suggest that students go back through the unit to review any words they have forgotten.
2. Have students check the skills they have mastered. If students need more practice to feel confident about their proficiency in a skill, point out the page numbers and encourage them to review.
3. Read the Learning Outcome aloud. Ask students if they feel that they have met the outcome.

Unit Assignment Rubric

Student name: ______________________________

Date: __________

Unit Assignment: Write a narrative essay.

20 points = Essay element was completely successful (at least 90% of the time).
15 points = Essay element was mostly successful (at least 70% of the time).
10 points = Essay element was partially successful (at least 50% of the time).
0 points = Essay element was not successful.

Write a Narrative Essay	20 points	15 points	10 points	0 points
Introduction tells who or what influenced the writer.				
Events are told in chronological order.				
Time words and time clauses are used correctly.				
The past perfect is used correctly.				
Essay includes correct punctuation, spelling, and grammar.				

Total points: __________

Comments:

UNIT 4

Unit QUESTION

How does the environment affect our health?

Health

READING • understanding purpose and text organization
VOCABULARY • synonyms
WRITING • organizing a five-paragraph essay
GRAMMAR • real conditionals

LEARNING OUTCOME

Identify and describe a harmful environmental issue and propose a possible solution to the problem.

Reading and Writing 4, pages 80–81

Preview the Unit

Learning Outcome

1. Ask for a volunteer to read the unit skills and the unit Learning Outcome.
2. Explain: *This is what you are expected to be able to do by the unit's end. The Learning Outcome explains how you are going to be evaluated. With this outcome in mind, you should focus on learning those skills (Reading, Vocabulary, Writing, Grammar) that will support your goal of describing a harmful environmental issue and proposing a solution to the problem. You can also act as a mentor in the classroom to help your classmates learn the skills and meet this Learning Outcome.*

A (15 minutes)

1. Tell students to look out the window (or to imagine what's outside). Ask: *What does the sky look like? Are there many trees? Is there a lot of trash on the ground? Do you think this (city/town/area) is clean?*
2. Put students in pairs or small groups to discuss the first two questions.
3. Call on volunteers to share their ideas with the class. Ask: *Are these environmental changes natural or caused by people? Do you think these changes are happening more quickly now than they did in the past? How has our environment in this city changed?*
4. Focus students' attention on the photo. Have a volunteer describe the photo to the class. Read the third question aloud. Elicit students' answers.

Preview the Unit A Answers, p. 81

Answers will vary. Sample answers:

1. In our city, there is more pollution now.
2. I think our city has a healthy environment. The water and air are clean. But, it can be dirty in the center of town because of the pollution from cars.
3. I think it is unhealthy to live in this environment. You would not want to breathe that air every day.

B (10 minutes)

1. Introduce the Unit Question: "How does the environment affect our health?" Ask related information questions or questions about personal experience to help students prepare for answering the more abstract Unit Question. For example, ask: *How do you feel when you are surrounded by nature compared to when you are in a big city? How can polluted water or air affect people?*
2. Put students in small groups and assign each group a different environmental problem (air pollution, water pollution, litter, etc.).
3. On a piece of paper, have them list ways that each problem can affect people's health. Encourage them to write as many ideas as they can think of.
4. Have groups share their ideas with the class. You may want to post the lists for students to refer back to later in the unit.

Preview the Unit B Answers, p 81

Answers will vary. Sample answers:
Lower-level answer: Dirty air can make us cough.
On-level answer: People who live in a clean environment are healthier than people who live in a polluted area.
Higher-level answer: Many people suffer health problems because of their environment. People who live in a big city where the air is polluted may have breathing problems or suffer from asthma.

The Q Classroom (5 minutes)

CD1, Track 11

1. Play *The Q Classroom*. Use the example from the audio to help students continue the conversation. Ask: *How did the students answer the question? Do you agree or disagree with their ideas? Why?*
2. Tell students to add any new environmental issues from the audio to their lists from Activity B.

Reading and Writing 4, page 82

C (10 minutes)

1. Read the directions. Do the first item as a class. Ask: *What do you see in this picture? What problems could you have with it that might affect your health?*
2. Have partners complete the activity.
3. Ask volunteers to share their ideas with the class.

Preview the Unit C Answers, p. 82

Answers will vary. Sample answers:

1. Dirty dishes in the sink could attract bugs or create germs that make people sick.
2. Toxic cleaning products could burn people's eyes or skin and cause breathing difficulties.
3. A dirty filter in the air conditioner may contain mold.
4. Unclean water can make people very sick.
5. Bacteria can grow on dirty laundry.
6. Gas stoves can sometimes have gas leaks.

MULTILEVEL OPTION

Elicit possible health problems from the class and make a list on the board. Lower-level students can complete Activity C using the list on the board.

D (10 minutes)

1. Call on students to read each idea.
2. Discuss if the idea was a new one, or if students had already thought of that idea.

Preview the Unit D Answers, p. 82

Answers will vary.

E (5 minutes)

Tell students to think of an answer before sharing it with a partner. Elicit ideas from the class.

Preview the Unit E Answers, p. 82

Answers will vary. Sample answer:

Another thing you can do to keep your home healthy is to be careful to refrigerate foods like meats or dairy products. Leaving these products at room temperature can cause bacteria to grow that may make people sick.

EXPANSION ACTIVITY: Informational Poster (20 minutes)

1. In pairs, have students choose one way that the environment can affect our health (for example, using toxic cleaning products) and make an informational poster about it.
2. On the board, list what the poster should include: title, picture, description of the problem (toxic cleaning products) and how it can affect our health (breathing problems, burning eyes, etc.).
3. Hang posters around the class and have students walk around to look at them. Invite students from other classes to view them as well.

READING

Reading and Writing 4, page 83

READING 1: Can Climate Change Make Us Sicker?

VOCABULARY (15 minutes)

1. Have students read each sentence and guess what the bold word means. Then have them write each word next to the correct definition.
2. Have students compare answers with a partner. Elicit answers from volunteers.

Vocabulary Answers, p. 83

a. implication; **b.** outbreak;
c. accelerated; **d.** annually;
e. consequence; **f.** statistics;
g. infiltrate; **h.** impact;
i. disrupt; **j.** media

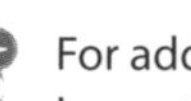

For additional practice with the vocabulary, have students visit *Q Online Practice*.

MULTILEVEL OPTION

Have higher-level students write additional sentences using the new vocabulary words. They can share their sentences with a partner while lower-level students complete the activity.

Reading and Writing 4, page 84

PREVIEW READING 1 (5 minutes)

1. Read the introduction. Elicit answers to the question and write them on the board.
2. Tell students they should review their answers after reading.

Preview Reading 1 Answer, p. 84
Answers will vary. Sample answer:
I think climate change can make us sicker because if the Earth gets warmer, there will be more diseases.

Reading 1 Background Note

Reading 1 discusses the broad, future effects of climate change, but what changes can we already see today?

The United States is seeing more wildfires sparked or fanned by rising temperatures. According to the National Interagency Fire Center, an average of 58 fires burned an average of 5,115,070 acres each year between 2001 and 2010.

Recently, there has been major flooding in Pakistan, caused by unusually strong storms. The BBC notes that the storm system contains the "worst monsoon rains" that Pakistan has seen in 80 years.

Mosquitoes thrive in hot weather, and as the planet heats up, more mosquitoes are being spotted for longer periods of time in places they were not seen before. For example, in 2007, England saw a large increase in its mosquito population during an August heat wave, which followed an unusually rainy spring. More mosquitoes mean more infectious diseases that humans will have to deal with.

READ (20 minutes)

CD1, Track 12

1. Instruct students to read the article. Remind them to refer to the glossed words as they read.
2. When students have finished, answer any questions they may have about the article or about additional vocabulary.
3. Play the audio and have students follow along.

Reading and Writing 4, page 86

MAIN IDEAS (10 minutes)

1. Have students read the statements and number the main ideas in the correct order. Direct them to go back to the article to underline the main idea in each paragraph.
2. Elicit the answers from volunteers.

Main Ideas Answers, p. 86
a. 2; **b.** 6; **c.** 4; **d.** 9; **e.** 1;
f. 5; **g.** 7; **h.** 3; **i.** 8

DETAILS (10 minutes)

1. Direct students to read the incomplete sentences and cross out the incorrect answer.
2. Have students compare answers with a partner. Remind them to look back at the article to check their answers.
3. Go over the answers with the class.

Details Answers, pp. 86-87
These items are incorrect (crossed out):
1. b; **2.** a; **3.** c; **4.** c; **5.** b; **6.** a

web For additional practice with reading comprehension, have students visit *Q Online Practice*.

Reading and Writing 4, page 87

WHAT DO YOU THINK? (20 minutes)

1. Ask students to read the questions and reflect on their answers.
2. Seat students in small groups and assign roles: a group leader to make sure everyone contributes, a note-taker to record the group's ideas, a reporter to share the group's ideas with the class, and a timekeeper to watch the clock.
3. Give students five minutes to discuss the questions. Call time if conversations are winding down. Allow them an extra minute or two if necessary.
4. Call on each group's reporter to share ideas with the class.
5. Have each student choose one of the questions and write a response for 5–10 minutes.
6. Call on volunteers to share their responses.

MULTILEVEL OPTION:

Have lower-level students work with a partner to respond to the same question.

As higher-level students finish writing, have them share their responses with a partner.

What Do You Think? Activity Answers, p. 87

Answers will vary. Sample answers:

1. Examples of extreme weather are very high or very low temperatures, tornadoes, typhoons, etc. Where I live, we have extremely high temperatures that sometimes start wildfires.
2. I live in a place that can have terrible floods. Climate change can make flooding worse, and people may suffer from health problems because of floods.
3. The government should educate people about what to do during floods, wildfires, etc.

Learning Outcome

Use the Learning Outcome to frame the purpose and relevance of Reading 1. Ask: *What did you learn from Reading 1 that prepares you to identify and describe a harmful environmental issue and propose a solution?* (Students learned about how climate change can affect our health. They may want to use some of the ideas from the article in their problem-solution essays.)

Reading and Writing 4, page 88

Reading Skill: Understanding purpose and text organization (10 minutes)

1. Have students read the information about understanding purpose. Check comprehension: *What are some common purposes of texts? How can you determine the purpose of a text?*
2. Discuss any texts or articles they have read in class that have one of the purposes listed.
3. Have students read the information about text organization. Check comprehension: *What are different ways to organize your ideas in a text?*

A (10 minutes)

1. Direct students to look back at Reading 1 to complete the activity.
2. Ask volunteers to share their answers with the class. Encourage students to support their answers with information from the article.

Reading Skill A Answers, p. 88

1. the effects of climate change on human health
2. to inform and persuade
3. problem and solution

Tip for Success (3 minutes)

1. Ask a volunteer to read the tip aloud.
2. Check comprehension by asking students what questions that texts with different purposes and organization would answer.

Reading and Writing 4, page 89

B (10 minutes)

1. Have students complete the chart with a partner.
2. Elicit answers from volunteers. Have students tell you where they found their answers in the article.

Reading Skill B Answers, p. 89

1. a. 300,000; b. may cause deaths of 500,000 per year
2. b. higher blood pressure in pregnant women;
   d. health issues in babies that can affect their hearts
3. a. mosquitoes living longer and moving into new areas; b. outbreaks of dengue fever

Critical Thinking Tip (2 minutes)

1. Have a student read the tip aloud.
2. Ask students to raise their hands if they think of themselves as "visual learners." Discuss how charts are helpful organizers. Point out any charts students have used or made in class.

C (10 minutes)

1. Read the directions aloud. Tell students to write at least two solutions that haven't been discussed.
2. Elicit solutions from volunteers. Write them on the board to compare and contrast.

Reading Skill C Answers, p. 89

Use technology to gather statistics on rainfall, temperature, and humidity.

Map out areas of potential outbreaks to prepare before they occur.

Use money now to deal with the health impacts of the hotter climate.

For additional practice with understanding purpose and text organization, have students visit *Q Online Practice*.

Critical Q: Expansion Activity

Identify and Evaluate Solutions

Direct students to identify environmental problems in their own communities and propose possible solutions. Have students brainstorm with a partner to list several local environmental issues. Elicit the issues from the class, and have each pair choose a different one to focus on.

Then have pairs propose and evaluate potential solutions to the problem. Have students note the advantages and disadvantages of each solution. Finally, have partners select the best solution for the problem and share their ideas with the class.

READING 2: Tips for a Greener Planet

VOCABULARY (15 minutes)

1. Read the directions and do the first item as a class. Help students identify the context clues (*family of four*) to help them get the answer: *as a group.*
2. Have students read each sentence and circle the correct definition. Remind them to use context clues to guess the meaning of each bold word. Encourage them to underline the context clues.
3. Elicit answers from volunteers.

Vocabulary Answers, pp. 89-90

1. b; **2.** a; **3.** a; **4.** b; **5.** b;
6. b; **7.** a; **8.** a; **9.** b; **10.** b

For additional practice with the vocabulary, have students visit *Q Online Practice*.

Reading and Writing 4, page 90

PREVIEW READING 2 (10 minutes)

1. Read the introduction aloud. Direct students to answer the questions.
2. Elicit answers from volunteers. Discuss any answers that are the same. Tell students they should review their answers after reading.

Preview Reading 2 Answers, p. 90

Answers will vary. Sample answers:

1. When I'm not feeling well, I try to rest at home. I also try to drink a lot of water and tea.
2. Something we do at home that is good for the planet is recycle. We separate our plastic bottles and paper products into separate bins.

Reading 2 Background Note

As Reading 2 suggests, there are changes every person can make to reduce their "carbon footprint." But how exactly does carbon dioxide lead to increases in global temperature?

As carbon dioxide gets released into the atmosphere—from cars, factories, and decaying plant life—it acts as a blanket, retaining the heat from the earth, but still allowing heat from the sun to reach the earth. As more carbon dioxide is released into the atmosphere, more of the earth's heat is trapped, therefore increasing the planet's temperature. If carbon dioxide levels are reduced, then more of the earth's heat would be released through the atmosphere and temperature levels would slowly decrease.

Reading and Writing 4, page 91

READ (20 minutes)

CD1, Track 13

1. Instruct students to read the article. Remind them to refer to the glossed words as they read.
2. When students have finished reading, answer any questions they may have about the article or about additional vocabulary.
3. Play the audio and have students follow along.

Reading and Writing 4, page 93

MAIN IDEAS (10 minutes)

1. Direct students to match the changes to the benefits. Tell them that some items have more than one answer.
2. Elicit the answers from volunteers. Then ask students to compare the main ideas from the article to their ideas in the Preview activity.

Main Ideas Answers, p. 93

1. c; **2.** e, h; **3.** a, f; **4.** b; **5.** d; **6.** g

Reading and Writing 4, page 94

DETAILS (10 minutes)

1. Direct students to label the statements *T* or *F*.
2. Have students compare answers with a partner. Remind them to look back at the article to check their answers.
3. Go over the answers with the class. Elicit corrections for the false statements.

Details Answers, p. 94

1. T;
2. F (A BRT system works best in less densely populated suburban areas.);
3. F (Companies with multiple locations in a single area would benefit from studying the commuting times of their employees.);
4. F (The typical U.S. household has shrunk from 3.4 to 2.6 inhabitants.);
5. T;
6. F (The number of people who describe themselves as "very happy" peaked in the 1950s.);
7. F (High-rise apartment buildings are easier to heat than individual homes.);
8. T

web For additional practice with reading comprehension, have students visit *Q Online Practice*.

WHAT DO YOU THINK?

A (15 minutes)

1. Ask students to read the questions and reflect on their answers.
2. Seat students in small groups and assign roles: a group leader to make sure everyone contributes, a note-taker to record the group's ideas, a reporter to share the group's ideas with the class, and a timekeeper to watch the clock.
3. Give students five minutes to discuss the questions. Call time if conversations are winding down. Allow them an extra minute or two if necessary.
4. Direct students to choose one question and write a paragraph in response.
5. Ask for volunteers to share their paragraph.

What Do You Think? Activity A Answers, p. 94

Answers will vary. Sample answers:

1. I am likely to live in a small home. I don't like big houses because there is more space to clean!
2. Another tip should be to drive less and take public transportation. Public transportation is less harmful to our environment.

B (10 minutes)

1. Tell the students that they should think about both Reading 1 and Reading 2 as they discuss the questions in Activity B.
2. Call on each group to share their answers.

What Do You Think? Activity B Answers, p. 94

Answers will vary. Sample answers:

1. Yes, because we should do our best to slow climate change and make the planet a better place to live.
2. Improving public health can improve individual health and vice versa because many illnesses are contagious. If we can prevent one person from getting sick, we may be able to prevent many people from getting sick. Also, if we can educate people about good health habits, the result is a more healthy population in general.

Learning Outcome

Use the Learning Outcome to frame the purpose and relevance of Readings 1 and 2. Ask: *What did you learn from Readings 1 and 2 that prepares you to identify and describe a harmful environmental issue and propose a solution?* (Students learned how environmental problems are harming people's health as well as what people can do to improve their own health and the health of the planet.)

Reading and Writing 4, page 95

Vocabulary Skill: Synonyms (10 minutes)

1. Ask volunteers to read the information about synonyms.
2. Check comprehension by asking: *What's a synonym? Can you think of a synonym for* problem? *Are all synonyms usually interchangeable?*
3. Provide additional examples of synonyms that differ in register (e.g., *dispose of* vs. *throw away*).
4. Discuss the subtle difference in meaning between *result* and *consequence.* Elicit any other synonym pairs that have a slight difference in meaning (e.g., *resident* vs. *citizen*).

Skill Note

Help students with using synonyms by teaching them how to use a thesaurus. Remind them that once they find a synonym, they should check the synonym's meaning in a dictionary to make sure it's appropriate. Remind them that synonyms often have slight differences in meaning, such as differences in formality, specificity, or connotation. For example, *assure* is more formal than *promise, portrait* is more specific than *picture,* and *stingy* is more negative than *frugal* or *economical.*

A useful exercise in a classroom where students share the same first language is to explore, briefly, synonyms in their first language. Do the synonyms mean exactly the same thing? This quick reflection will help students understand that synonyms in all languages differ slightly in meaning and register.

A (15 minutes)

1. Read the directions aloud. Direct students to complete the activity individually.
2. Go over the answers with the class. Discuss any differences in meaning between the synonyms.

Vocabulary Skill A Answers, pp. 95–96

2. neglected; **3.** cause; **4.** effect; **5.** improve; **6.** vehicles; **7.** commute; **8.** contented; **9.** consume; **10.** reduced

Tip for Success (1 minute)

1. Ask for a volunteer to read the tip aloud.
2. Explain: *When you are writing, use a thesaurus to find synonyms for words that you are using too often or that have a general meaning (e.g. happy, nice, big, etc.) Be sure to check the meaning of the synonym in the dictionary to make sure it is appropriate for the context of your writing.*

21ST CENTURY SKILLS

Employers want employees who know how to use resources independently to find the answers or information they need. Point out to students that in both the classroom and the workplace, there will be times when they will need to search for answers or information themselves. Knowing where to look and what resources to use to find that information is an important skill.

Teaching students how to use a dictionary and thesaurus helps them achieve learner independence and gives them access to life-long resources. Remind students that learning to use resources to find answers, rather than relying on others, will make them more independent learners and workers. Encourage students to find answers to their own questions in the class. When they ask what something means or how to spell something, help them to find the answer on their own.

▶ *Reading and Writing 4, page 96*

B (15 minutes)

1. Direct students to write their sentences individually. Help them craft sentences that show the synonyms' nuances in meaning.
2. Ask for volunteers to write their sentences on the board. Discuss the differences in meaning of the synonyms with the class.

Vocabulary Skill B Answers, p. 96

Answers will vary. Sample sentences:

1. Learning a foreign language can really enrich your life. / I want to improve my understanding of how to write an essay.
2. I can't wear my favorite shirt anymore because it shrunk when I washed it in hot water. / Having a dryer has really reduced the amount of time it takes to do laundry.
3. I try not to consume more than one or two cans of soda per week. / I often use an electric tea kettle to boil water.

For additional practice with synonyms, have students visit Q Online Practice.

▶ *Reading and Writing 4, page 97*

WRITING

Writing Skill: Writing a five-paragraph essay (25 minutes)

1. Read the information about the elements of a five-paragraph essay. Pause to summarize and allow students to ask questions after each section.
2. Check comprehension. Ask: *What are the parts of the introduction? What should each body paragraph include? What does a conclusion do?*
3. Direct students to read the essay and complete the activities on page 98.
4. Have them compare answers with a partner. Elicit answers from the class. You may want to project the paragraph to show the answers.

Writing Skill Answers, p. 98

1. "Think green!' We have all heard this slogan many times, but do we understand what it means? Three ways we can help both ourselves and the planet are (1) to turn off the electronics, (2) plant a vegetable garden, and (3) support green projects.
2. Body Para 1: A great way to "think green" is to turn off the electronics in our homes and spend time doing other activities instead of watching TV or surfing the Internet. We can choose activities that not only interest us but are also kind to the planet.
   Body Para 2: One idea is to plant a vegetable garden, which will help both the gardener and the planet. Gardening is one small way to go green and relieve stress....
   Body Para 3: It is also important to support green projects that help the planet. Supporting and participating in green projects is healthy for us and the planet.
3. Body Para 1: ✓ So what is a good way to use this free time?
   Body Para 2: ✓ . . . but you can also encourage environmental responsibility in bigger ways.
4. ✓ restates the thesis statement in different words.
   ✓ predicts what will happen in the future.
5. Answers will vary.

Tip for Success (1 minute)

1. Ask for a volunteer to read the tip aloud.
2. Explain: *In longer essays, unity and cohesion become more important in order to keep the essay focused and the reader on track.*

For additional practice with writing a five-paragraph essay, have students visit *Q Online Practice.*

Reading and Writing 4, page 99

Grammar: Real conditionals (10 minutes)

1. Read the information about real conditionals and the example sentences in the first chart. Check comprehension. Ask: *When are real conditionals used? When do you need to use a comma? What is an example of a sentence with an if-clause?* Elicit additional examples of real conditionals.
2. Go over the subordinators in the second chart, highlighting the differences in meaning. Provide additional sentences using the subordinators.

Skill Note

Present and future real conditionals express possible situations or events and their results. However, by changing the verb in the main clause, sentences can have slightly different meanings. For example, *If I have time, I will/might plant a garden.*

The first two examples on page 99 about ice melting express general truths. The third example, with *going to* (*will* could also be used here), expresses future plans with a strong result. The fourth example with *can* has a slightly weakened result, expressing a future possibility.

Other modals that express less certain results are *should, may,* and *might*. For example, *If it rains tomorrow, I may go to the movies.*

A (15 minutes)

1. Direct students to read the directions and complete the activity individually.
2. Have pairs discuss the sentences they found.
3. Elicit the sentences from volunteers.

Grammar A Answers, p. 99

1. Our actions may not feel very significant when we act alone. Only if many individuals make changes in their behavior collectively can the power of this change be....
2. ...if more Americans leave their cars at home, there will be much less pollution and better air quality.
3. Even if people drive less, they still need to get from point A to point B.
4. Unless you already live in a big urban area, you may not think of a city as a green place to live.
5. When you're packed together with your neighbors, it's easier to find a community of friends who.... If you feel connected to others and don't feel "all alone in the big city," your health improves, too. Even if you are sometimes annoyed by your noisy neighbors, you can be happy that you are helping the planet by sharing space!

Reading and Writing 4, page 100

B (10 minutes)

1. Have students complete the sentences.
2. Ask volunteers to put their sentences on the board. Correct the sentences as a class.

Grammar B Answers, p. 100

Answers will vary. Sample answers:

2. We will be able to make better decisions if we educate ourselves.
3. Even if you don't notice climate change every day, it is real.
4. Only if we work together can we solve global problems.
5. Unless we all make changes in our lives, we can't prevent climate change.
6. You can live a green lifestyle as long as you're willing to change.

For additional practice with real conditionals, have students visit *Q Online Practice.*

Unit Assignment:
Write a five-paragraph problem and solution essay

Unit Question (5 minutes)

Refer students back to the ideas they discussed at the beginning of the unit about how the environment can affect our health. Cue students if necessary by asking specific questions about the content of the unit: *What are some of the environmental problems we have discussed? What kinds of health problems can be caused by environmental problems?*

Learning Outcome

1. Tie the Unit Assignment to the unit Learning Outcome. Say: *The outcome for this unit is to write a five-paragraph problem and solution essay. This Unit Assignment is going to let you show your skill in writing a problem and solution essay with real conditional sentences.*
2. Explain that you are going to use a rubric similar to their Self-Assessment checklist on p. 102 to grade their Unit Assignment. You can also share a copy of the Unit Assignment Rubric (on p. 45 of this *Teacher's Handbook*) with the students.

Plan and Write

Brainstorm

A (15 minutes)

1. Direct students to brainstorm with a partner.
2. Explain that the purpose of brainstorming is to write down as many ideas as possible. Remind students to write notes instead of sentences.
3. Suggest that students add a third column to their chart to note possible solutions.

▶ *Reading and Writing 4, page 101*

Tip for Success (1 minute)

1. Ask for a volunteer to read the tip aloud.
2. Explain to students that it's a good idea to wait until they've finished writing the essay to write the hook. That way, they'll know exactly what is in the essay and what they should refer to in order to get the reader's attention.

Plan

B (20 minutes)

1. Tell students to use their ideas from Activity A to complete the outline.
2. Monitor and provide feedback.

▶ *Reading and Writing 4, page 102*

Write

C (20 minutes)

1. Review the Self-Assessment checklist on p. 102. Tell students to use their outline from Activity B to write their essay.
2. Remind them to use real conditional sentences.

Alternative Unit Assignments

Assign or have students choose one of these assignments to do instead of, or in addition to, the Unit Assignment.

1. Write a five-paragraph essay in which you identify a problem in education, give reasons for the problem, and offer possible solutions.
2. Write a five-paragraph essay explaining what you do for your health and the planet's health.

For an additional Unit Assignment, have students visit *Q Online Practice.*

Revise and Edit

Peer Review

A (15 minutes)

1. Pair students and have them read each other's work
2. Have students answer and discuss the questions.
3. Give students suggestions of helpful feedback: *You are missing a possible solution in paragraph 2. I liked your hook; it made me laugh. There's a problem with the if-clause in this sentence.*

Rewrite

B (10 minutes)

Students should review their partners' answers from Activity A and rewrite their essays if necessary.

Edit

C (10 minutes)

1. Direct students to read and complete the Self-Assessment checklist. They should be prepared to hand in their work or discuss it in class.
2. Ask for a show of hands for how many students gave all or mostly yes answers.
3. Use the Unit Assignment Rubric on p. 45 in this *Teacher's Handbook* to score each student's assignment.
4. Alternatively, divide the class into large groups and have students read their essays to their group. Pass out copies of the Unit Assignment Rubric and have students grade each other.

Reading and Writing 4, page 103

Track Your Success (5 minutes)

1. Have students circle the words they have learned in this unit. Suggest that students go back through the unit to review any words they have forgotten.
2. Have students check the skills they have mastered. If students need more practice to feel confident about their proficiency in a skill, point out the page numbers and encourage them to review.
3. Read the Learning Outcome aloud. Ask students if they feel that they have met the outcome.

Unit Assignment Rubric

Student name: ____________________

Date: __________

Unit Assignment: *Write a five-paragraph problem and solution essay.*

20 points = Essay element was completely successful (at least 90% of the time).
15 points = Essay element was mostly successful (at least 70% of the time).
10 points = Essay element was partially successful (at least 50% of the time).
0 points = Essay element was not successful.

Write a Five-Paragraph Problem and Solution Essay	20 points	15 points	10 points	0 points
Essay describes an environmental issue, gives three related health problems, and proposes possible solutions.				
Essay includes an introduction, three body paragraphs, and a conclusion.				
Each body paragraph explains a health problem.				
Real conditional sentences are used correctly.				
Punctuation, spelling, and grammar are used correctly.				

Total points: __________

Comments:

UNIT 5

Unit QUESTION

How important is art?

Art Today

READING • compare and contrast organization
VOCABULARY • using the dictionary to learn homonyms
WRITING • writing a compare and contrast essay
GRAMMAR • subordinators and transitions to compare and contrast

LEARNING OUTCOME

Compare and contrast two artists, performers, or works of art that share an interesting relationship.

Reading and Writing 4, pages 105–106

Preview the Unit

Learning Outcome

1. Ask for a volunteer to read the unit skills and the unit Learning Outcome.
2. Explain: *This is what you are expected to be able to do by the unit's end. The Learning Outcome explains how you are going to be evaluated. With this outcome in mind, you should focus on learning those skills (Reading, Vocabulary, Writing, Grammar) that will support your goal of comparing and contrasting two artists, performers, or works of art that share an interesting relationship. You can also act as a mentor in the classroom to help your classmates learn the skills and meet this Learning Outcome.*

A (15 minutes)

1. Ask students: *What do you consider to be art? Do you create any art? If so, what do you make?*
2. Put students in pairs or small groups to discuss the first two questions.
3. Have volunteers share their ideas with the class. Ask: *What would life be like without art?*
4. Focus students' attention on the photo. Have a volunteer describe the photo to the class. Read the third question aloud. Elicit students' answers.

Preview the Unit A Answers, p. 105

Answers will vary. Sample answers:

1. I like painting because there are different styles.
2. I think that people become professional artists because they want to express themselves. It's difficult for many artists to make enough money.
3. People in a museum are taking pictures of the famous painting "The Mona Lisa."

B (15 minutes)

1. Introduce the Unit Question: *How important is art?* Ask related information questions or questions about personal experience to help students prepare for answering the more abstract Unit Question. For example, ask: *What do people like about art? What does art tell us about ourselves or our cultures?*
2. Read the Unit Question aloud. Point out that students may answer that art is important or that it's not important. Give students a minute to silently consider their answers to the question.
3. At the top of two sheets of poster paper, write *It's important because…* and *It's not important because…* Elicit answers to the Unit Question and make notes of the answers under the correct headings. Post the lists to refer to later in the unit.

Preview the Unit B Answers, p. 105

Answers will vary. Sample answers:
Lower-level answer: Art is important because it is beautiful. / Art is not important because it's just something nice to look at.
On-level answer: Art is important because people can express themselves. / Art is not important because people should learn more valuable things.
Higher-level answer: Art is important because it gives people the chance to express themselves. / Art is not important because it doesn't teach people the skills they need to live in today's world.

The Q Classroom (5 minutes)

CD1, Track 14

1. Play *The Q Classroom*. Use the example from the audio to help students continue the conversation. Ask: *How did the students answer the question? Do you agree or disagree with their ideas? Why?*

2. Write on the board: *Is art a luxury, or is it necessary?* Have students discuss the question. Elicit answers from volunteers.

Reading and Writing 4, page 106

C (10 minutes)

1. Read through the quotations and answer any questions about unknown vocabulary.
2. Direct students to complete the task in pairs.

Preview the Unit C Answers, p. 106

1. Answers will vary. Sample answers: (1) A writer should paint pictures with words and a painter should write words with pictures; (2) An artist is a person who makes luxury goods; (3) When looking at art, we see both the familiar and the strange at the same time; (4) Art allows us to escape the everyday world by using our imagination;(5) Creativity is spontaneous and natural; (6) A talented actor needs very little to become anyone or anything.
2. Answers will vary.

D (10 minutes)

1. Have students discuss their answers in groups.
2. Call on each group to share their ideas.

MULTILEVEL OPTION

Put students in mixed-ability groups to discuss their answers. This way, higher-level students will be able to provide lower-level students with key vocabulary as they discuss the quotations.

Preview the Unit D Answers, p. 106

Answers will vary.

EXPANSION ACTIVITY: Classmate Survey (10 minutes)

1. Direct students to choose their favorite quotation from p. 106 and survey at least four classmates about it.
2. Remind students to read their quotation aloud and ask their classmates why they agree or disagree.
3. Call on students to share their classmates' responses with the class.

READING

Reading and Writing 4, page 107

READING 1: Two Styles of Songwriting

VOCABULARY (15 minutes)

1. Have students read each sentence, guess what the word in bold means, and write the word next to the correct definition.
2. Elicit answers from volunteers.
3. Pronounce each word and have students repeat.

MULTILEVEL OPTION

Pair lower-level students and assist them with the task. Provide alternate example sentences to help them understand the words. For example, *The student* ***tackled*** *the difficult math problem. I can always* ***count on*** *my sister to help me. Learning English will help me* ***in the long run*** *because I will be able to get a better job.*

Have higher-level students write an additional sentence for each word. Ask students to write their sentences on the board. Correct the sentences as a class, focusing on the use of the words and expressions rather than other grammatical issues.

Vocabulary Answers, pp. 107-108

a. burn out; **b.** inferior; **c.** talent; **d.** instinct; **e.** undertake; **f.** inspire; **g.** essentially; **h.** in the long run; **i.** tackle; **j.** tedious; **k.** craft; **l.** count on

For additional practice with the vocabulary, have students visit *Q Online Practice*.

Reading and Writing 4, page 108

PREVIEW READING 1 (5 minutes)

1. Read the introduction. Preview the methods and direct students to check those they might use.
2. Tell students to review their answers after reading.

Preview Reading 1 Answer, p. 108

Answers will vary.

Reading 1 Background Note

Songwriting is a lucrative business. Here are short biographies of a few successful, modern songwriters.

Pat Alger is an American songwriter who has written many successful songs for country music artists. His song credits include "When the Thunder Rolls" by Garth Brooks and "Small Town Saturday Night" by Trisha Yearwood. He has also seen his songs recorded by performers such as Dolly Parton. He was inducted into the Nashville Songwriters Hall of Fame in 2010.

Kate Bush is a songwriter from Kent, England. She began her recording career in 1978 and has recorded singles such as "Wuthering Heights" and "Running up that Hill." She recently received an award recognizing her contributions to British music.

Reading and Writing 4, page 109

READ (20 minutes)

CD1 Track 15

1. Instruct students to read the excerpt. Remind them to refer to the glossed words as they read.
2. When students have finished, answer any questions about the excerpt or vocabulary. Then play the audio and have students follow along.

Reading and Writing 4, page 111

MAIN IDEAS (10 minutes)

1. Have students complete the activity individually.
2. Check the answers as a class.

Main Ideas Answers, p. 111

1. c; **2.** b; **3.** c; **4.** b; **5.** a

DETAILS (10 minutes)

1. Direct students to label the statements *T* or *F*.
2. Have students compare answers with a partner.
3. Go over the answers with the class. Elicit corrections for the false statements.

Details Answers, p. 111

1. F; **2.** F; **3.** F; **4.** T;
5. F; **6.** F; **7.** T; **8.** F

For additional practice with reading comprehension, have students visit *Q Online Practice.*

Reading and Writing 4, page 112

WHAT DO YOU THINK? (20 minutes)

1. Ask students to read the questions and reflect on their answers.
2. Seat students in small groups and assign roles: a group leader to make sure everyone contributes, a note-taker to record the group's ideas, a reporter to share the group's ideas with the class, and a timekeeper to watch the clock.
3. Give students five minutes to discuss the questions. Call time if conversations are winding down. Allow them an extra minute or two if necessary.
4. Call on each group's reporter to share ideas with the class.
5. Have each student choose one of the questions and write a response for 5–10 minutes.
6. Call on volunteers to share their responses.

What Do You Think? Activity Answers, p. 112

Answers will vary. Sample answers:

1. An artist is someone with creative talent. Artists rely more on instinct, but they can also learn new skills.
2. I rely more on inspiration than craft when solving a creative problem. Some things must be decided by the heart.

Learning Outcome

Use the Learning Outcome to frame the purpose and relevance of Reading 1. Ask: *What did you learn from Reading 1 that prepares you to compare and contrast two artists, performers, or works of art that share an interesting relationship?* (Students learned about two different approaches to songwriting.)

Reading Skill: Understanding compare and contrast organization (15 minutes)

1. Read the information about understanding compare and contrast organization. Point out how the underlined information in the paragraph can be organized in a T-chart.
2. Check comprehension: *Why do writers compare and contrast information? What is a* T-chart *and why would you use one?*

Tip for Success (1 minute)

1. Read the tip aloud. Direct students to look at p. 88.
2. Explain: *Knowing how the information in a text is organized will help you understand the text.*

▶ *Reading and Writing 4, page 113*

Critical Thinking Tip (1 minute)

Read the tip aloud. Then explain: *Putting information into categories helps you to compare and contrast. When you decide which category an idea belongs in, you think critically about that idea in relation to other ideas.*

A (10 minutes)

1. Read the directions aloud. Ask: *Can you remember any good or bad points from the reading?*
2. Direct students to reread the paragraphs and complete the chart individually.

Reading Skill A Answers, p. 113

Answers will vary. Sample answers:

Craft writers' good points: can reveal hidden talent; write about a wide variety of subjects; help find new ways to say things; can become a better writer, problem solver; write lots of songs

Craft writers' bad points: writing may become boring, not fun; songs don't sound enjoyable; can become lazy or repetitive; may produce inferior material; may cause problems for other writers

Instinctive writers' good points: don't know what will happen next; it's magical to write this way; no pressure of deadlines; rely on their talent; often find new ways to say things

Instinctive writers' bad points: don't pay attention to craft; success can be frightening; never know if they'll be able to write; cannot work with deadlines; cannot improve their work

B (10 minutes)

1. Have students discuss their chart with a partner and fill in any points they missed.
2. Ask volunteers to share their answers with the class as you recreate the chart on the board.

Reading Skill B Answers, p. 113

Answers will vary.

For additional practice with understanding compare and contrast organization, have students visit *Q Online Practice.*

READING 2: What Does It Take to Be a Successful Artist?

VOCABULARY (15 minutes)

1. As students read each sentence, encourage them to guess what they think the word in bold means before they circle the correct answer.
2. Elicit answers from volunteers. Pronounce each bold word and have students repeat.

Vocabulary Answers, pp. 113-114

1. a; **2.** c; **3.** b; **4.** b; **5.** a; **6.** c;
7. a; **8.** c; **9.** c; **10.** b; **11.** a; **12.** c

MULTILEVEL OPTION

Pair lower-level students and assist them with the task. Provide alternate example sentences to help them understand the words. For example, *I* ***devote*** *4 hours a week to studying English. The house* ***stood out*** *on the street because it was pink.*

Have higher-level students write an additional sentence for each vocabulary word. Ask students to write their sentences on the board. Correct the sentences as a class, focusing on the use of the words and expressions rather than other grammatical issues.

For additional practice with the vocabulary, have students visit *Q Online Practice.*

▶ *Reading and Writing 4, page 114*

PREVIEW READING 2 (5 minutes)

1. Read the introduction aloud. Have students write three qualities to answer the question.
2. Tell students to review their ideas after reading.

Preview Reading 2 Answers, p. 114

Answers will vary. Sample answers:

creativity / passion / vision/ knowledge / confidence / technical skills (drawing, painting, etc.)

Reading 2 Background Note

The New York Times calls Ralph Fasanella, one of the artists in the reading, "a self-taught, folk-primitive artist who created bold, colorful compositions loaded with minute detail."

Born to Italian immigrants, he spent his childhood helping his father deliver ice. He discovered painting in his 30s, when a co-worker suggested that painting might be a way to relieve the arthritis pain in his hands. The subjects he chose to paint were city and work life because he was a union member and wanted to depict the life of average, working Americans.

However, Fasanella was nearly 60 when his art became popular. Working as a painter for almost 30 years before his "breakthrough," his story shows it can take a lot of time to become a successful artist.

▶ *Reading and Writing 4, page 115*

READ (20 minutes)

CD1, Track 16

1. Instruct students to read the excerpt. Remind them to refer to the glossed words as they read.
2. When students have finished, answer any questions about the excerpt or vocabulary. Then play the audio and have students follow along.

▶ *Reading and Writing 4, page 117*

MAIN IDEAS (10 minutes)

1. Read the directions aloud. Direct students to complete the activity individually and then compare answers with a partner.
2. Elicit answers from the class.

Main Ideas Answers, p. 117

Successful artists . . .

1. ✗ Paragraph 3 (They don't care if their art sells.)
2. ✓ Paragraph 4 (To the true artist, the task at hand is the only thing that matters.)
3. ✓ Paragraph 8 (To be sure, most art experts put self-confidence on top of their list of desirable characteristics.)
4. ✗ Paragraph 1 (The amateur rarely has it.)
5. ✓ Paragraph 7 (Many artists have refused to marry or, after neglecting their families, suffered divorces.)
6. ✓ Paragraph 3 (This single-minded purpose, this deep affection for art, turns up in the stories of most major artists.)
7. ✓ Paragraph 1 (Is it possible that successful artists share certain character traits? They probably do.)
8. ✗ Paragraph 5 (When he was painting, Church would row himself as close as possible to the icebergs so that he could make a realistic drawing of the falling ice.) and 7 (one such experiment hurt her so badly she had to have two operations on her hand.)

Tip for Success (2 minutes)

1. Read the tip aloud. Explain: *When you scan a text, set a time limit so you don't read the whole text.*
2. Tell students that scanning the reading for names will help them complete the Details Activity.

▶ *Reading and Writing 4, page 118*

DETAILS (5 minutes)

Have students match the artists to the descriptions. Then go over the answers with the class.

Details Answers, p. 118

1. f; **2.** b; **3.** e; **4.** g; **5.** d; **6.** c; **7.** a

MULTILEVEL OPTION

Pair lower-level students for this activity. They may take longer than higher-level students to scan the text.

web For additional practice with reading comprehension, have students visit *Q Online Practice*.

WHAT DO YOU THINK?

A (15 minutes)

1. Ask students to read the questions and reflect on their answers.
2. Seat students in small groups and assign roles: a group leader to make sure everyone contributes, a note-taker to record the group's ideas, a reporter to share the group's ideas with the class, and a timekeeper to watch the clock.
3. Give students five minutes to discuss the questions. Call time if conversations are winding down. Allow them an extra minute or two if necessary.
4. Then have students choose one question and write a paragraph in response.
5. Call on volunteers to share their responses.

What Do You Think? Activity A Answers, p. 118

Answers will vary. Sample answers:

1. The author of Reading 2 says that successful authors have passion and persistence. I think I have persistence because when I start something that is important to me, I always try to finish it.
2. Yes, I agree. If artists don't focus and get distracted by other things, they might not be successful.

B (10 minutes)

1. Tell students that they should think about both Reading 1 and Reading 2 as they answer the questions in Activity B.
2. Give students five minutes to discuss the questions. Call time if conversations are winding down. Allow them an extra minute or two if necessary.
3. Call on each group to share ideas with the class.

What Do You Think? Activity B Answers, p. 118

Answers will vary. Sample answers:

1. The author of Reading 2 would say that craft is more important than inspiration. He talks a lot about artists' dedication. The author of Reading 1 says a craft writer is someone who "writes from 9 to 5." Reading 2 gives many examples of artists who put in long hours at their craft.
2. Yes, because some people are just born with great talent. I think there are many musicians who have no formal training but create wonderful music.

Critical Q: Expansion Activity

Identify Characteristics of Artists

Pair students and provide them with poster paper and a marker. Direct them to make a word web that shows the characteristics of successful artists from Reading 2. If students are unfamiliar with this type of graphic organizer, model creating a simple word web on the board for a similar topic, such as *Characteristics of a Student*.

Have students review Reading 2 to identify the characteristics and record them in their web. Then have pairs share their webs with other pairs, comparing and contrasting the contents.

Create a web on the board and elicit characteristics from the class. Help students with any vocabulary that might come up in trying to describe the characteristics.

Learning Outcome

Use the Learning Outcome to frame the purpose and relevance of Readings 1 and 2 and the Critical Q expansion activity. Ask: *What did you learn from Readings 1 and 2 that prepares you to compare and contrast two artists, performers, or works of art that share an interesting relationship?* (Students learned about some artists' approaches to their craft and common characteristics that artists share. This will help them as they write their essays.)

▶ *Reading and Writing 4, page 119*

Vocabulary Skill: Using the dictionary

(10 minutes)

Ask volunteers to read the information about homonyms. Then check comprehension. Ask: *What is a homonym? What homonyms do you know?*

Skill Note

Strict homonyms are words that are spelled the same but have different meanings (*bow* – a thing used to play string instruments; *bow* – what you tie in your shoelaces). However, the term *homonym* also includes homophones, which are words that sound the same but are spelled differently (e.g. *through, threw*). If you add the word *bow* (to move your body or head downward) to the examples above, you have a *heteronym*, or a word with a different meaning that is spelled the same but pronounced differently.

A (5 minutes)

1. Have students complete the activity individually.
2. Elicit answers from volunteers. Discuss the parts of speech that *craft* can be. Elicit additional sentences using the word.

Vocabulary Skill A Answers, p. 119

1. a noun, a verb; **2.** a boat; a skill; to make

▶ *Reading and Writing 4, page 120*

B (15 minutes)

1. Ask a volunteer to read the directions aloud. Direct students to complete the activity individually and then compare answers with a partner.
2. Elicit answers from the class.

Vocabulary Skills B Answers, p. 120

Answers will vary. Sample answers from the *Oxford Advanced American Dictionary for Learners of English:*

1. noun: all the skills needed for a particular activity
2. noun: a way of dealing with somebody or something; a way of doing or thinking about something, such as a problem or task
3. noun: a thing or person that is being discussed, described, or dealt with
4. noun: difficulties or feelings of anxiety that are caused by the need to achieve or to behave in a particular way
5. verb: to have the same feelings, ideas, experiences, etc. as somebody else
6. idiom: (have something in common) to have the same interests, ideas, etc. as somebody else
7. adjective: very large or important
8. noun: things that are needed in order to do a particular activity

For additional practice with homonyms, have students visit *Q Online Practice*.

Reading and Writing 4, page 121

WRITING

Writing Skill: Writing a compare and contrast essay (15 minutes)

1. Read the information about writing and organizing a compare and contrast essay. Pause to summarize. Allow students to ask questions after each section.
2. Check comprehension: *What should you include in the introduction? What is one way to organize your body paragraphs? What does the conclusion do?*

A (15 minutes)

1. Direct students to read the essay and answer the questions. Have partners compare answers.
2. Elicit answers from volunteers.

Writing Skills A Answers, p. 122

1. Thesis: Although Norah Jones was born 20 years after Billie Holiday died, Jones's music can be similar to Holiday's.
2. The essay is organized point by point.
3. To evenly balance the essay between two subjects.

Reading and Writing 4, page 123

B (10 minutes)

1. Ask a volunteer to read the directions aloud.
2. Students should complete the chart and then compare their answers with a partner.
3. Recreate the chart on the board and have students fill it in.

Writing Skills B Answers, p. 123

Billie Holiday

Life: tough childhood; successful; famous; very poor; won Grammy awards

Training: no musical training; learned from musicians around her

Music: sings only jazz; sings quiet, emotional songs; writes and sings; not well known as a songwriter

Norah Jones

Life: parents famous musician and dancer; successful; famous; attended good schools; won Grammy awards

Training: studied piano and jazz piano; no training as a singer; learned singing from musicians and recordings

Music: sings jazz, country and pop; sings quiet, emotional songs; some songs are faster; writes and sings; well known as a songwriter

C (10 minutes)

1. Have partners work together to complete the chart. Remind them that this is a different way to organize the same information from Activity B.
2. Ask: *Which chart (B or C) do you like better? How would you prefer to organize your compare and contrast essay? Why?*

Writing Skills C Answers, p. 123

Similarities: successful; famous; won Grammy awards; no training as a singer; learned from musicians around her; sings quiet, emotional songs; writes and sings

Differences:

Billie Holiday: tough childhood; very poor; sings only jazz; not well known as a songwriter

Norah Jones: parents famous musician and dancer; studied piano and jazz piano; sings jazz, country and pop; well known as a songwriter

For additional practice with writing a compare and contrast essay, have students visit *Q Online Practice*.

21ST CENTURY SKILLS

Comparing and contrasting requires students to think critically about an item and its relationship to something else. In the workplace, they might be asked to compare two solutions to a problem or two items for a customer. Point out that businesses always have to compare and contrast ideas when thinking about any new approach or strategy. In short, successful people are always comparing and contrasting two—or sometimes more—options to discover which option might be the better one.

Reading and Writing 4, page 124

Grammar: Subordinators and transitions to compare and contrast (15 minutes)

1. Read the information about subordinators that show contrast. Ask: *What are some examples of subordinators that show contrast?* Point out that sentences with *although, though,* and *while* convey the meaning of "Yes, but…."
2. Elicit additional sentences using *whereas, while, although,* or *though.*

3. Read the information about transitions showing comparison and contrast. Check comprehension: *What are some examples of transitions that show comparison? Contrast?*
4. Pair students and challenge them to think of another sentence using one of the transition words.

Skill Note

The subordinators *although* and *though* can be used interchangeably at the beginning of a sentence. However, only *though* can be used at the end of a sentence. *Though* is also used in the adverbial phrases *even though* and *as though.*

The transitions *in spite of this* and *despite this* must be used when both clauses of a sentence refer to the same person. For example, *Holiday had no musical training. In spite of this, she was a gifted singer.*

Reading and Writing 4, page 125

A (10 minutes)

1. Model doing the first item for the students.
2. Have students complete the activity individually and then elicit answers from volunteers.

Grammar A Answers, p. 125

1. whereas, CT;
2. on the other hand, CT;
3. Similarly, CP;
4. Likewise, CP;
5. however, CT

B (10 minutes)

1. Have students complete the activity individually and then compare answers with a partner.
2. Elicit the answers from volunteers.

Grammar B Answers, p. 125

1. plays better than Julio;
2. only plays on weekends;
3. plays songs by other artists;
4. it as much as the piano;
5. Julio is always working on something new;
6. only Frieda wants to do it professionally

C (10 minutes)

1. Direct students to complete the sentences.
2. Ask a few students to write their sentences on the board. Elicit additional sentences from the class.

Grammar C Answers, pp. 125–126

Answers will vary. Sample answers:

2. Although many people enjoy art, many others don't think art is important.
3. Not many people become professional artists. Likewise, few people become professional singers.
4. Musicians often have rigorous training. On the other hand, some very famous musicians have had no training.
5. I like both Norah Jones and Billie Holiday. However I think I prefer Billie Holiday's style.
6. Whereas some craft writers may burn out, instinctive writers may never finish a song.
7. Artists need ambition to succeed. Similarly, people in business do not succeed without ambition.

web For additional practice with subordinators and transitions to compare and contrast, have students visit *Q Online Practice.*

Reading and Writing 4, page 126

Unit Assignment: Write a compare and contrast essay

Unit Question (5 minutes)

Refer students back to the ideas they discussed at the beginning of the unit about the importance of art. Cue students by asking specific questions about the content of the unit: *Why do people like art? What do some artists do to become successful?*

Learning Outcome

1. Tie the Unit Assignment to the unit Learning Outcome. Say: *The outcome for this unit is to write a five-paragraph essay comparing and contrasting two artists, performers, or works of art. This Unit Assignment is going to let you show your skill in writing an essay with subordinators and transitions that compare and contrast.*
2. Explain that you are going to use a rubric similar to their Self-Assessment checklist on p. 128 to grade their Unit Assignment. You can also share a copy of the Unit Assignment Rubric (on p. 55 of this *Teacher's Handbook*) with the students.

Plan and Write

Brainstorm

A (15 minutes)

1. Direct students to follow the steps with a partner.
2. Remind them to make notes in their charts rather than writing in complete sentences.

Tip for Success (1 minute)

1. Ask a volunteer to read the tip aloud. Refer students back to the two charts on p. 123.
2. Remind them that the charts show the same information in different ways. Tell students to choose the chart that seems most appropriate.

▶ *Reading and Writing 4, page 127*

Plan

B (20 minutes)

Students should use their charts from Activity A to write their outlines. Monitor and provide feedback on their outlines.

Tip for Success (1 minute)

1. Ask a volunteer to read the tip aloud.
2. Tell students: *Often the last thing we read or the last thing we see in a movie sticks out in our minds. For this reason, it's a good idea to build toward your strongest argument or most interesting idea.*

Write

C (20 minutes)

1. Review the Self-Assessment checklist on p. 128.
2. Direct students to write their essays.

Alternative Unit Assignments

Assign or have students choose one of these assignments to do instead of, or in addition to, the Unit Assignment.

1. Which would you rather do—read a book or watch a movie based on the book? Write an essay comparing the two experiences.
2. Write an essay comparing the work of two artists. The two artists can work in the same field (e.g., two actors, two musicians, etc.) or different fields.

For an additional Unit Assignment, have students visit *Q Online Practice*.

▶ *Reading and Writing 4, page 128*

Revise and Edit

Peer Review

A (15 minutes)

1. Pair students and direct them to read each other's work.
2. Ask students to answer and discuss the questions.
3. Give students suggestions of helpful feedback: *Your concluding sentence was very strong. I think you could use a transition here to show contrast.*

Rewrite

B (10 minutes)

Students should review their partners' answers from Activity A and rewrite their paragraphs if necessary.

Write

C (10 minutes)

1. Direct students to read and complete the Self-Assessment checklist. They should be prepared to hand in their work or discuss it in class.
2. Ask for a show of hands for how many students gave all or mostly *yes* answers.
3. Use the Unit Assignment Rubric on p. 55 in this *Teacher's Handbook* to score each student's assignment.
4. Alternatively, divide the class into large groups and have students read their paragraphs to their group. Pass out copies of the Unit Assignment Rubric and have students grade each other.

▶ *Reading and Writing 4, page 129*

Track Your Success (5 minutes)

1. Have students circle the words they have learned in this unit. Suggest that students go back through the unit to review any words they have forgotten.
2. Have students check the skills they have mastered. If students need more practice to feel confident about the proficiency in a skill, point out the page numbers and encourage them to review.
3. Read the Learning Outcome aloud. Ask students if they feel that they have met the outcome.

Unit Assignment Rubric

Student name: ______________________________

Date: __________

Unit Assignment: *Write a compare and contrast essay.*

20 points = Essay element was completely successful (at least 90% of the time).
15 points = Essay element was mostly successful (at least 70% of the time).
10 points = Essay element was partially successful (at least 50% of the time).
0 points = Essay element was not successful.

Write a Compare and Contrast Essay	20 points	15 points	10 points	0 points
Essay tells why it is important to compare and contrast the two subjects.				
Essay is organized using one of the compare and contrast essay types.				
Essay includes an introduction, three body paragraphs, and a conclusion.				
Essay includes subordinators and transitions that compare and contrast.				
Punctuation, spelling, and grammar are correct.				

Total points: __________

Comments:

UNIT 6

Unit QUESTION
Should science influence what we eat?

The Science of Food

READING • recognizing bias
VOCABULARY • cause and effect collocations
WRITING • writing a cause and effect essay
GRAMMAR • agents with the passive voice

LEARNING OUTCOME

Express your opinions about the positive or negative effects of science on the food we eat.

Reading and Writing 4, pages 130–131

Preview the Unit

Learning Outcome

1. Ask for a volunteer to read the unit skills and the unit Learning Outcome.
2. Explain: *This is what you are expected to be able to do by the unit's end. The Learning Outcome explains how you are going to be evaluated. With this outcome in mind, you should focus on learning those skills (Reading, Vocabulary, Writing, Grammar) that will support your goal of expressing your opinion about the positive or negative effects of science on the food we eat. You can also act as a mentor and help your classmates learn the skills to achieve this Learning Outcome.*

A (15 minutes)

1. Ask students: *What does it mean to be healthy? What foods do you think are good for you? Is your health important to you? Why?*
2. Put students in pairs or small groups to discuss the first two questions.
3. Elicit ideas from volunteers. List what students have eaten today. Ask questions: *Is this food healthy? What should there be more or less of?*
4. Focus students' attention on the photo. Have a volunteer describe the photo to the class. Read the third question aloud. Elicit students' answers. Keep a tally of how many students say *yes* or *no*.

Preview the Unit A Answers, p. 131

Answers will vary. Sample answers:

1. Yes, I think I have a healthy diet. Sometimes I eat sweets, but I don't eat them every day.
2. Eating for pleasure is more important to me because food is one of the most enjoyable things in life.
3. Yes, because the food looks clean and safe.

B (15 minutes)

1. Introduce the Unit Question: "Should science influence what we eat?" Ask related information questions or questions about personal experience to help students prepare for answering the more abstract Unit Question. For example, ask: *How do scientists know what is healthy? Have you heard that margarine is healthier than butter (or vice versa)? When you hear information like this, do you change what you eat? Why or why not?*
2. Read the Unit Question aloud. Give students a minute to silently consider their answers to the question. Ask students who would answer *yes* to stand on one side of the room and students who would answer *no* to stand on the other side.
3. Direct students to tell the person next to them their reasons for choosing the answer they did.
4. Call on volunteers from each side to share their opinions with the class.
5. After students have shared their opinions, provide an opportunity for anyone who would like to change sides to do so.
6. Ask students to sit down, copy the Unit Question, and make a note of their answers and their reasons. They will refer back to these notes at the end of the unit.

Preview the Unit B Answers, p. 131

Answers will vary. Sample answers:
Lower-level answer: Yes, because scientists know more about food than most people.
On-level answer: I think scientific information can help people improve their diet. Scientists know how different foods affect our bodies.
Higher-level answer: People should consider scientific information when making choices about their diets. Scientists have studied how certain foods affect our bodies and health, and we should listen to their advice.

The Q Classroom **(5 minutes)**

CD2, Track 2

1. Play *The Q Classroom*. Use the example from the audio to help students continue the conversation. Ask: *How did the students answer the question? Do you agree or disagree with their ideas? Why?*
2. Ask students to write 2–3 sentences explaining their current opinion. Tell them they should look back at this opinion at the end of the unit.

► ***Reading and Writing 4, page 132***

C (15 minutes)

1. Tell students that there is a lot of false information about things that are healthy (or not). In Activity C, they will decide whether a statement is true (a fact) or false (a myth).
2. Direct students to complete the questionnaire and then compare answers with a partner.
3. Have students check their answers against the answer key. Ask them which answers surprised them the most.

MULTILEVEL OPTION

Higher-level students can write a brief summary of their reaction to the questionnaire. They should discuss which facts and myths surprised them and why. They should also include whether or not this information will change their eating habits.

Preview the Unit C Answers, p. 132

1. Myth; **2.** Myth; **3.** Fact; **4.** Myth;
5. Fact; **6.** Myth; **7.** Myth; **8.** Myth

EXPANSION ACTIVITY: Food Fact or Myth? (20 minutes)

1. Tell students that they will expand upon the questionnaire by writing their own "Fact or Myth?" statements.
2. Elicit any other ideas about food that students know about (e.g. margarine is better than butter; it's good to eat lemons and garlic when you don't feel well; etc.).
3. Have students write down a statement about food and survey their classmates to see if they believe the statement is a fact or a myth.
4. Then have students research their statements and report back to the class.

READING

► ***Reading and Writing 4, page 133***

READING 1: Eating Well: Less Science, More Common Sense

VOCABULARY (15 minutes)

1. Have students read the vocabulary words and their definitions. Read each word aloud and have students repeat. Highlight the syllable that receives primary stress in each word.
2. Direct students to complete the sentences with the bold words.
3. Call on volunteers to read the sentences. Ask students to point out the context clues that helped them choose each word.

MULTILEVEL OPTION

Group lower-level students and assist them with the task. Provide additional sentences using the vocabulary words. For example, *I would like to try to* ***eliminate*** *soft drinks from my diet. If your low-fat diet isn't working, you should try a different* ***approach,*** *like eating a low-carbohydrate diet. One* ***benefit*** *of not having a car is that I get a lot of exercise by walking everywhere.*

Have higher-level students write an additional sentence for each word. Ask students to write their sentences on the board. Correct the sentences with the class, focusing on the use of the words rather than other grammatical issues.

Vocabulary Answers, pp. 133–134

1. eliminate; **2.** expert;
3. benefit; **4.** link;
5. access; **6.** participate;
7. finding; **8.** encourage;
9. practical; **10.** approach;
11. physical; **12.** challenge

For additional practice with the vocabulary, have students visit *Q Online Practice*.

► ***Reading and Writing 4, page 134***

PREVIEW READING 1 (10 minutes)

1. Direct students to read the introduction and answer the questions individually.
2. Tell students they should review their answers after reading.

Preview Reading 1 Answer, p. 134

1. No, the author does not think science should help us choose the foods we eat. He thinks common sense should.
2. Answers will vary. Possible answer: The author may suggest that we use common sense, rather than science, when deciding what to eat. Looking at the picture, I think the author believes food labels can be confusing.

Tip for Success (5 minutes)

1. Ask for a volunteer to read the tip aloud.
2. Look at several examples of words in italics and quotation marks from this textbook or another. Discuss what is being emphasized.

Reading and Writing 4, page 135

Reading 1 Background Note

Michael Pollan is a professor, author, and food activist. Pollan has written many books on the subject of food and health and argues that the modern agricultural industry has lost touch with the food chain as nature intended.

Pollan's critics argue that his stance is not based in science, a claim that Pollan agrees with. He blames science for society's modern health issues. Pollan's critics also assert that his criticism of the food industry does not take cost into account.

READ (20 minutes)

CD2 Track 3

1. Instruct students to read the article. Remind them to refer to the glossed words as they read.
2. When students have finished reading, answer any questions students may have about the article or additional vocabulary.
3. Play the audio and have students follow along.

Reading and Writing 4, page 137

MAIN IDEAS (10 minutes)

1. Direct students to mark the statements *Y* or *N*.
2. Elicit answers from volunteers. Ask students to support their answers with information from the article.

Main Ideas Answers, p. 137

1. N; **2.** N; **3.** Y; **4.** Y; **5.** N; **6.** Y

DETAILS

A (5 minutes)

1. Direct students to circle the best answer to each question.
2. Have students compare answers with a partner. Remind them to look back at the article to check their answers.
3. Go over the answers with the class.

Details A Answers, pp. 137–138

1. c; **2.** a; **3.** b; **4.** b; **5.** c

Reading and Writing 4, page 138

B (10 minutes)

1. Direct students to go back to the article and underline the benefits of having an urban garden.
2. Have students compare their answers with a partner. Then elicit the answers from volunteers.

Details B Answers, p. 138

1. People are healthier. / They have access to more fresh fruit and vegetables, especially poorer people.
2. The food costs less than it would in a supermarket.
3. People get exercise.
4. Working together in the garden promotes community and sharing.

web For additional practice with reading comprehension, have students visit *Q Online Practice*.

WHAT DO YOU THINK? (20 minutes)

1. Ask students to read the questions and reflect on their answers.
2. Seat students in small groups and assign roles: a group leader to make sure everyone contributes, a note-taker to record the group's ideas, a reporter to share the group's ideas with the class, and a timekeeper to watch the clock.
3. Give students five minutes to discuss the questions. Call time if conversations are winding down. Allow them an extra minute or two if necessary.
4. Call on each group's reporter to share ideas with the class.
5. Have each student choose one of the questions and write a response to it for 5–10 minutes.
6. Call on volunteers to share their responses.

MULTILEVEL OPTION:

For question 2, allow lower-level students to list foods they've eaten rather than write in complete sentences.

What Do You Think? Activity Answers, p. 138

Answers will vary. Sample answers:

1. I don't usually pay attention to the results of scientific studies. Some advice that I do take seriously is to eat margarine instead of butter. I understand that butter is worse for my health.
2. Three meals I have eaten lately are: rice with chicken, a ham sandwich, and beet soup with potatoes. This food is not mostly plants, but most of it was fresh. I try to shop at the outdoor market instead of the supermarket, but sometimes I have to do what is most convenient.
3. Another benefit of an urban garden is that it creates an open, green space in the middle of buildings and concrete.

Learning Outcome

Use the Learning Outcome to frame the purpose and relevance of Reading 1. Ask: *What did you learn from Reading 1 that prepares you to express your opinions about the positive or negative effects of science on the food we eat?* (Students read about the challenges people face when trying to make healthy choices about food. They may want to refer to these ideas when they write their cause and effect essays.)

Reading Skill: Recognizing bias (10 minutes)

1. Call on students to read the information about recognizing bias.
2. Check comprehension: *What is bias? Why is it important to recognize bias? What are some techniques writers use to influence their readers? Have you ever read an article by someone who had a particular bias?*

▶ *Reading and Writing 4, page 139*

A (10 minutes)

1. Have partners read the sentences to determine which technique is used. Remind them that some sentences may have two answers.
2. Elicit answers from volunteers.

Reading Skill A Answers, p. 139

a. 2, 4; **b.** 1; **c.** 2, 3; **d.** 3;
e. 4; **f.** 2, 4; **g.** 2, 4; **h.** 1

Critical Thinking Tip (1 minute)

1. Read the tip aloud.
2. Explain: *As you read, look out for words or techniques that the writer uses to persuade the reader. This will help you figure out how the writer feels about the topic.*

▶ *Reading and Writing 4, page 140*

Tip for Success (1 minute)

1. Ask for a volunteer to read the tip aloud.
2. Explain: *Once you determine a writer's bias, look carefully at the text to make sure the writer's opinion is supported by reasons and examples.*

B (10 minutes)

1. Have students work with their partners from Activity A to complete the activity.
2. Elicit answers from volunteers. Refer back to the techniques on pp. 138-139. You may want to project the page to show the underlining.

Reading Skill B Answers, p. 140

Answers will vary. Sample answers:

a. 2; You may have read that my colleagues do not agree with me on this topic. But let me make this clear: my colleagues have ignored the latest research data.
b. 3; Not all fats are bad for you. In reality, some are very good for you.
c. 1; Nutrition advice can sometimes be difficult to understand.
d. 4; We are all concerned about our weight getting out of control, so let's do something about it.
e. 3; Research into nutrition has been going on for decades, but in fact, much is still unknown about foods as simple as the carrot.
f. You and I both know that candy isn't good for our teeth, so why do we continue to eat it?
g. 1; You won't believe how delicious the cheesecake is: it's an absolute miracle.
h. 2; Everyone wants to eat healthily. Many food manufacturers, however, are more interested in keeping costs down than in using healthy ingredients.

For additional practice with recognizing bias, have students visit *Q Online Practice*.

READING 2:
Anatomy of a Nutrition Trend

VOCABULARY (15 minutes)

1. Have students read the vocabulary words and their definitions. Say each word for students to repeat.
2. Direct students to complete the paragraph by filling in the blanks with the vocabulary words.
3. Ask volunteers to read the paragraph aloud.

Vocabulary Answers, p. 141

1. milestone;	**2.** contribute;
3. Currently;	**4.** primarily;
5. shift;	**6.** source;
7. modify;	**8.** major;
9. stable;	**10.** sink in

For additional practice with the vocabulary, have students visit *Q Online Practice*.

Reading and Writing 4, page 141
PREVIEW READING 2 (5 minutes)

1. Read the introduction and have students check their answer. Discuss their answers as a class.
2. Tell students to review their answers after reading.

Preview Reading 2 Answer, p. 141
Answers will vary.

Reading 2 Background Note

Low-carbohydrate diets are popular because they help people lose weight. However, doctors warn people against eating this way over an extended period of time. Because people on low-carb diets avoid carbohydrates, they tend to increase the amount of protein (especially meat) they are consuming. Increased fat intake from so much protein can be unhealthy for people's heart and may increase their cholesterol levels.

Reading and Writing 4, page 142
READ (20 minutes)

CD2, Track 4

1. Instruct students to read the article. Remind them to refer to the glossed words as they read.
2. When students have finished reading, answer any questions they may have about the article or additional vocabulary.
3. Play the audio and have students follow along.

Reading and Writing 4, page 144
MAIN IDEAS (15 minutes)

1. Direct students to answer the questions.
2. Have them compare answers with a partner, checking their answers against the article.
3. Elicit answers from volunteers.

Main Ideas Answers, p. 144

1. A new book or new scientific research
2. A food recall or when people die from a food-related disease
3. *Two of the following:* beliefs about what keeps us healthy, attitudes about our ability to control our health, reactions to hearing stories and reading books, talking with friends and family
4. From the media and primarily from magazines
5. Repetition—hearing the same thing from a number of sources
6. The health benefits that certain foods may provide (functional foods)

Reading and Writing 4, page 145
DETAILS (10 minutes)

1. Direct students to read the statements and check the correct source.
2. Have students compare answers with a partner. Remind them to look back at the article to check their answers.
3. Go over the answers with the class.

Details Answers, p. 145

1. Felicia Busch;
2. FMI;
3. Linda Gilbert;
4. FMI;
5. Linda Gilbert;
6. Felicia Busch;
7. IFIC Foundation;
8. Felicia Busch

For additional practice with reading comprehension, have students visit *Q Online Practice*.

WHAT DO YOU THINK?

A (15 minutes)

1. Ask students to read the questions and reflect on their answers.
2. Seat students in small groups and assign roles: a group leader to make sure everyone contributes, a note-taker to record the group's ideas, a reporter to share the group's ideas with the class, and a timekeeper to watch the clock.
3. Give students five minutes to discuss the questions. Call time if conversations are winding down. Allow them an extra minute or two if necessary.
4. Call on each group's reporter to share ideas with the class.
5. Have each student choose one of the questions and write a paragraph in response.
6. Call on volunteers to share their responses.

What Do You Think? Activity A Answers, p. 145

Answers will vary. Sample answers:

1. I trust information from health care providers most. They are trained to understand research and medicine.
2. Trends in nutrition are different from trends in music or fashion because what we eat can greatly affect our health. Trying a new style of clothing or type of music is not nearly as risky as changing our eating habits.

▶ *Reading and Writing 4, page 146*

B (10 minutes)

1. Tell the students that they should think about both Reading 1 and Reading 2 as they answer the questions in Activity B.
2. Call on each group's reporter to give a brief summary of the group's discussion.

What Do You Think? Activity B Answers, p. 146

Answers will vary. Sample answers:

1. I don't think the author of Reading 1 will be successful in changing people's minds about science and food because people mostly get their nutritional information from the media. The media seems to love stories about food trends and diet advice, so people do too.
2. In Reading 1, the author is expressing his opinion and trying to change our minds. In Reading 2, the author presents information from different sources. I think Reading 2 is more objective because it doesn't present just one person's opinion.

Critical Q: Expansion Activity

Analyze for Bias

To recognize an author's bias, students should first ask themselves *Who is the audience for the article?* Understanding who the author is speaking to can help students think about the author's intentions. Second, students should ask *What are the author's beliefs on this topic?* Students should use the techniques on pp. 138-139 to recognize bias and identify the author's opinions and beliefs.

To practice the process of analyzing for bias, ask students to think about their decision-making process for answering Question 2 on p. 146. Ask: *How did you determine which author was more objective? What evidence did you find and analyze to support your conclusion?*

Learning Outcome

Use the Learning Outcome to frame the purpose and relevance of Readings 1 and 2. Ask: *What did you learn from Readings 1 and 2 that prepares you to express your opinions about the positive or negative effects of science on the food we eat?* (Students read about how consumers can make healthy choices without depending on research and how nutritional trends get started. They may want to refer to some of these ideas in their cause and effect essays.)

Vocabulary Skill: Cause and effect collocations (10 minutes)

1. Call on volunteers to read the information aloud.
2. Check comprehension: *What's a collocation? What are some collocations you can use when the cause/effect is the subject of the sentence?*

Skill Note

When students learn a new word, they should try to become aware of the word's register, part of speech, multiple meanings, and collocations. Have students make checking for collocations a part of their process for learning new vocabulary. When introducing new words, draw students' attention to other words that collocate with the new vocabulary. For example, point out that the word *contribute* in this unit collocates with the preposition *to,* as in *Scientific research contributes to our understanding of healthy foods.* The *Oxford Collocations Dictionary* has over 250,000 collocations and 75,000 examples for students of English.

A (5 minutes)

1. Direct students to complete each sentence with a collocation from the skill box.
2. Have them compare answers with a partner.
3. Elicit answers from volunteers. Discuss any slight differences in meaning among the collocations.

Vocabulary Skill A Answers, p. 146

Answers will vary. Sample answers:

1. Tiredness and stress **are responsible for** many traffic accidents
2. Greenhouse gases **lead to** global warming.
3. A good diet **contributes to** excellent health.
4. Poverty **is a factor** in much of the crime in our society.
5. Eric's carelessness **brought about** his injury.
6. The poor economy **resulted in** the failure of the company last year.

Reading and Writing 4, page 147

B (5 minutes)

1. Direct students to write a different collocation in each blank and then compare answers with a partner.
2. Elicit answers from volunteers. Discuss any differences in answers that students have.

Vocabulary Skill B Answers, p. 147

Answers will vary. Sample answers:

1. Sylvie's good grades **are due to** her excellent memory.
2. The hotel fire **was caused by** an electrical problem.
3. My fight with my brother **arose from** a misunderstanding.
4. The high price of gas **stems from** a petroleum shortage.
5. Harry's love of art **developed from** a childhood trip to the museum.
6. The success of the movie **came from** the great action scenes.

web For additional practice with cause and effect collocations, have students visit *Q Online Practice.*

C (15 minutes)

1. Direct students to work with a partner to write six cause and effect sentences.
2. Have volunteers write sentences on the board. Go over the sentences as a class, focusing on the use of the collocations.

Vocabulary Skill C Answers, p. 147

Answers will vary. Sample sentences:

Cause as subject: Smoking can bring about many health problems. / Eating more fruits and vegetables can lead to a stronger immune system. / Eating a good breakfast can be a factor in how children perform at school.

Effect as subject: People's concern about their diet can stem from a desire to live longer. / People's confusion about what to eat may be due to the fact that scientists' advice changes often. / My dream to be a dietician was brought about by my parents' unhealthy eating choices.

Reading and Writing 4, page 148

WRITING

Writing Skill: Writing a cause and effect essay (10 minutes)

1. Tell students that they will write a new kind of essay: the cause and effect essay. Read the information together.
2. Check comprehension: *What does a cause and effect essay do? What are two ways to organize the essay? What are the three parts of a cause and effect essay?*

21ST CENTURY SKILLS

Explain to students that understanding cause and effect relationships is a skill that can also help them in the workplace. For example, they may need to think about the potential results of an important business decision or explain the possible causes of a current problem. As a class, discuss workplace situations in which students might need to identify a cause or effect.

Reading and Writing 4, page 149

A (15 minutes)

1. Direct students to read the essay and answer the questions.
2. Have students compare their answers with a partner before asking for volunteers to share their answers with the class.

Writing Skill A Answers, p. 149

1. The causes of an issue
2. Answer will vary, but may include facts, examples, explanations, descriptions, etc.
3. Any answer focusing on lack of mental control

▶ *Reading and Writing 4, page 150*

B (15 minutes)

1. Have partners fill in the outline together.
2. Elicit answers from volunteers. You may want to copy the outline on the board.

Writing Skill B Answers, p. 150

Answers will vary. Sample answers:

I. Thesis statement: We can't lose weight because of the way we think about food.

II. Cause 1: People don't follow the plan.
A. Support 1: They change diets frequently.
B. Support 2: They become discouraged if the weight doesn't go away fast.

III. Cause 2: The stress of modern life leads to comfort eating.
A. Support 1: We eat when we feel down. / We use food as an escape.
B. Support 2: We use food as a reward.

IV. Cause 3: We also need to look closely at the food we eat and read food labels.
A. Support 1: Low-fat foods may contain other fattening substances.
B. Support 2: Some low-fat foods may not have much fat taken out.

V. Concluding advice: Control your mind and you can control your body.

web For additional practice with writing a cause and effect essay, have students visit *Q Online Practice*.

Grammar: Agents with the passive voice (10 minutes)

1. Have students read the information about the passive voice. Discuss the grammar point as a class. Highlight the difference in the verbs in the active and passive sentences.
2. Check comprehension: *What is an agent? How is the passive formed?* Elicit additional examples of passive sentences.

Skill Note

It is important that students understand not only how to form the passive but also its purpose. The passive voice is used to emphasize the person or thing affected by the action. For example, in the sentence *The study was conducted by Dr. Barnes,* the study is given more importance than the person (agent), Dr. Barnes, who conducted it. It is likely that the next sentence will discuss information in the study, rather than information about Dr. Barnes.

▶ *Reading and Writing 4, page 151*

A (10 minutes)

1. Direct students to read the sentences and complete the activity.
2. Have partners compare their answers.
3. Elicit the answers from volunteers. Discuss why the agent is important (or not) in each sentence.

Grammar A Answers, p. 151

Obvious agents to be deleted:

1. ~~by a salesclerk;~~
2. ✓;
3. ~~by the delivery guy;~~
4. ✓;
5. ✓;
6. ~~by the doctor;~~
7. ~~by the audience;~~
8. ✓;
9. ✓;
10. ~~by people~~

B (10 minutes)

1. Have partners complete the activity together.
2. Go over the answers with the class. Discuss why an agent is needed (or not) in each sentence.

Grammar B Answers, pp. 151–152

Answers will vary. Sample answers:

1. That house is going to be repainted.
2. In my favorite restaurant, all the food is prepared by the owner.
3. My computer is being repaired.
4. The accident victim was taken to the hospital.
5. Many famous painters are influenced by other artists.
6. I was trying to get to sleep, but I was disturbed by a noise from the street.
7. Everyone was shocked when the office was broken into.
8. After the author's death, his novel was finished by his son.

Tip for Success (1 minute)

1. Read the tip aloud.
2. Explain: *An agent is only necessary when it provides specific information about who is doing the action. It is not necessary to include an agent if it is obvious who is doing the action.*

For additional practice with agents with the passive voice, have students visit *Q Online Practice*.

▶ *Reading and Writing 4, page 152*

Unit Assignment: Write a cause and effect essay

Unit Question (5 minutes)

Refer students back to the ideas they discussed at the beginning of the unit about the influence of science on the food we eat. Cue students if necessary by asking specific questions about the content of the unit: *What are some positive effects of science on the food we eat? What are some negative effects? What would the author of Reading 1 say about letting science influence our diet?*

Learning Outcome

1. Tie the Unit Assignment to the unit Learning Outcome. Say: *The outcome for this unit is to write a cause and effect essay. This Unit Assignment is going to let you show your skill in writing an essay that includes cause and effect collocations and the passive voice.*
2. Explain that you are going to use a rubric similar to their Self-Assessment checklist on p. 154 to grade their Unit Assignment. You can also share a copy of the Unit Assignment Rubric (on p. 66 of this *Teacher's Handbook*) with the students.

Plan and Write

Brainstorm

A (15 minutes)

Direct students to work with a partner to complete the chart and discuss their ideas.

▶ *Reading and Writing 4, page 153*

Plan

B (20 minutes)

1. Tell students to use their notes from Activity A to write an outline for their essay.
2. Direct students to work individually. They may talk to a partner if they need help thinking of details to support each effect.

Tip for Success (1 minute)

1. Ask a volunteer to read the tip aloud.
2. Explain: *Unity is what connects your ideas together. Every effect should be related to your thesis statement, and every detail should clearly support an effect.*

Write

C (20 minutes)

1. Before students begin writing, have them look at the Self-Assessment checklist on page 154.
2. Remind students to include cause and effect collocations from p. 147 in their essay.

Alternative Unit Assignments

Assign or have students choose one of these assignments to do instead of, or in addition to, the Unit Assignment.

1. Write a five-paragraph cause and effect essay on the topic, "The advantages and disadvantages of fast food." Include cause and effect collocations and the passive where appropriate.
2. If you disagreed with Michael Pollan's views in Reading 1, write a response explaining your own opinions. Use research or evidence from your own experience to support your views.

For an additional Unit Assignment, have students visit *Q Online Practice*.

▶ *Reading and Writing 4, page 154*

Revise and Edit

Peer Review

A (15 minutes)

1. Pair students and direct them to read each other's work
2. Ask students to answer and discuss the questions.
3. Give students suggestions of helpful feedback: *Your essay is well-organized. You should include more cause and effect collocations. Add another supporting detail in the second paragraph.*

Rewrite

B (10 minutes)

Students should review their partners' answers from A and rewrite their paragraphs if necessary.

Edit

C (10 minutes)

1. Direct students to read and complete the Self-Assessment checklist. They should be prepared to hand in their work or discuss it in class.
2. Ask for a show of hands for how many students gave all or mostly *yes* answers.
3. Use the Unit Assignment Rubric on p. 66 in this *Teacher's Handbook* to score each student's essay.
4. Alternatively, divide the class into large groups and have students read their essay to their group. Pass out copies of the Unit Assignment Rubric and have students grade each other.

Reading and Writing 4, page 155

Track Your Success (5 minutes)

1. Have students circle the words they have learned in this unit. Suggest that students go back through the unit to review any words they have forgotten.
2. Have students check the skills they have mastered. If students need more practice to feel confident about their proficiency in a skill, point out the page number and encourage them to review.
3. Read the Learning Outcome aloud. Ask students if they feel that they have met the outcome.

Unit Assignment Rubric

Student name: ______________________________

Date: __________

Unit Assignment: *Write a cause and effect essay.*

20 points = Essay element was completely successful (at least 90% of the time).
15 points = Essay element was mostly successful (at least 70% of the time).
10 points = Essay element was partially successful (at least 50% of the time).
0 points = Essay element was not successful.

Write a Cause and Effect Essay	20 points	15 points	10 points	0 points
Essay clearly describes three effects of science on food we eat.				
Each effect is supported by facts, examples, or descriptions.				
Essay includes an introduction, three body paragraphs, and a conclusion.				
Passive verbs are used correctly.				
Cause and effect collocations are used correctly.				

Total points: __________

Comments:

UNIT 7

Unit QUESTION

Does school prepare you for work?

Work and Education

READING • using an outline
VOCABULARY • word forms
WRITING • writing a summary
GRAMMAR • reported speech with the present tense

LEARNING OUTCOME

Summarize and paraphrase the purpose, thesis statement, main ideas, and conclusions of a text.

Reading and Writing 4, pages 156–157

Preview the Unit

Learning Outcome

1. Ask for a volunteer to read the unit skills and the unit Learning Outcome.
2. Explain: *This is what you are expected to be able to do by the unit's end. The Learning Outcome explains how you are going to be evaluated. With this outcome in mind, you should focus on learning those skills (Reading, Vocabulary, Writing, Grammar) that will support your goal of summarizing the important points of a text. You can also act as a mentor in the classroom to help your classmates learn the skills and meet this Learning Outcome.*

A (15 minutes)

1. Tell students to think back to their school years. Ask: *What were your goals? What classes did you take? What do you remember learning?*
2. Put students in pairs or small groups to discuss the first two questions.
3. Call on volunteers to share their ideas. Ask: *What is something about adult life that you didn't imagine when you were younger? What has changed now that you are an adult? What is something that you think school should have taught you?*
4. Focus students' attention on the photo. Have a volunteer describe the photo. Read the third question aloud. Elicit answers from students.

Preview the Unit A Answers, p. 157

Answers will vary. Sample answers:

1. Students learn to work independently, think critically, and ask questions. These skills can help them in their careers.
2. I think parents help students the most. They teach them to be responsible and to do what is right.
3. It's a good way to get people's attention and tell them you want a job, but I don't think you can find a real job this way.

B (15 minutes)

1. Introduce the Unit Question: "Does school prepare you for work?" Ask related information questions or questions about personal experience to help students prepare for answering the more abstract Unit Question. Ask: *What kind of skills or knowledge do you need for your job now? Did you learn any of these in school?*
2. Read the Unit Question aloud. Give students a minute to silently consider their answers to the question. Then ask students who would answer *yes* to stand on one side of the room and students who would answer *no* to stand on the other side.
3. Direct students to tell the person next to them their reasons for choosing the answer they did.
4. Call on volunteers from each side to share their opinions with the class.
5. After students have shared their opinions, provide an opportunity for anyone who would like to change sides to do so.
6. Ask students to sit down, copy the Unit Question, and make a note of their answers and reasons. They will refer back to these notes at the end of the unit.

Preview the Unit B Answers, p. 157

Answers will vary. Sample answers:
Lower-level answer: No, because in school you learn a lot of information that you won't use in your job.
On-level answer: No, because in school you have to study many subjects, but you probably won't need a lot of this information in your future job.
Higher-level answer: No, because students have to study subjects like physics and history, which they will probably never use in their jobs. Also, you don't usually work in groups in school, but you often have to work with others in your job.

The Q Classroom (5 minutes)

CD2, Track 5

1. Play *The Q Classroom*. Use the example from the audio to help students continue the conversation. Ask: *How did the students answer the question? Do you agree or disagree with their ideas? Why?*
2. Have students write a short response explaining which student from the listening they agree with the most.

Reading and Writing 4, page 158

C (10 minutes)

1. Tell students to read the list of skills. Clarify any difficult words, such as *consistently* or *efficiently*.
2. Have partners discuss the questions together.

Preview the Unit C Answers, p. 158

Answers will vary. Sample answers:

1. I would add "Work independently" to the list of school skills. I would remove "Asks teachers for clarification" because I don't think students are expected to do that often.
2. Finishing homework on time helps students learn to meet deadlines in their future jobs. / Interacting with peers socially may help students network with others effectively in the future.

MULTILEVEL OPTION

Place students in mixed-ability pairs as they complete Activity C. Higher-level students can help explain vocabulary words or provide examples as the pair works together to answer the questions. Then have higher-level students from each group lead the discussion in Activity D.

D (10 minutes)

Have partners discuss their answers with another pair. Then elicit answers from volunteers.

Preview the Unit D Answers, p. 158

Answers will vary.

EXPANSION ACTIVITY: Discuss Skills (15 minutes)

1. From the list on page 158, assign each pair one skill needed to succeed in school. Have them brainstorm why they need this skill in school.
2. Then have each pair discuss how the skill could be useful at work. They should think of at least two or three examples from the workplace.
3. Have each pair describe their skill and how it is used in the classroom and workplace. Ask other students to add to their classmates' examples.

READING

Reading and Writing 4, page 159

READING 1:
From Student to Employee

VOCABULARY (15 minutes)

1. Direct students to read each sentence and guess the meaning of the word in bold before circling the correct answer.
2. Elicit answers from volunteers.

MULTILEVEL OPTION

Pair lower-level students and assist them with the task. Provide alternate example sentences to help them understand the words. For example: *The noise from the workers was* ***constant.*** *It never stopped. If you come from a hot country, it can be difficult to* ***adjust*** *to cold winters. The school project was* ***collaborative,*** *so the students worked in teams.*

Instruct higher-level students to write additional sentences with the vocabulary words. Ask volunteers to write their sentences on the board. As you go over the activity answers, use the higher-level students' sentences as additional examples of context.

Vocabulary Answers, pp. 159–160

1. c;	**2.** c;	**3.** b;	**4.** b;
5. c;	**6.** b;	**7.** c;	**8.** a;
9. c;	**10.** a;	**11.** a;	**12.** b

web For additional practice with the vocabulary, have students visit *Q Online Practice*.

▶ *Reading and Writing 4, page 160*

PREVIEW READING 1 (10 minutes)

1. Read the introduction aloud. Then have students answer the questions.
2. Tell students they should review their answers after reading.

Preview Reading 1 Answers, p. 160

Answers will vary. Sample answers:

1. The author probably thinks that making the transition from student to employee is a difficult time in a person's life.
2. Maybe the author had a difficult time getting a full-time job after graduation.

Reading 1 Background Note

The website *BetterHighSchools.org* supports the argument made by the author of Reading 1 that school does not sufficiently prepare students for their future employment. Much research indicates that schools' goals need to be more closely aligned with the goals of students' future employers. This means that the curriculum taught in high schools should include the knowledge and skills that will likely be needed in students' first jobs.

Many researchers also suggest that high schools need to collaborate with employers. This may include school-workplace partnerships that allow students to gain work experience before graduating and entering the "real world."

READ (20 minutes)

CD2 Track 6

1. Instruct students to read the article. Remind them to refer to the glossed words as they read.
2. When students have finished reading, answer any questions about the article or additional vocabulary.
3. Play the audio and have students follow along.

▶ *Reading and Writing 4, page 162*

MAIN IDEAS (10 minutes)

1. Have students complete the activity individually.
2. Elicit answers from volunteers.

Main Ideas Answers, pp. 162–163

1. c; **2.** c; **3.** b; **4.** a; **5.** a; **6.** b

▶ *Reading and Writing 4, page 163*

Reading Skill: Using an outline (5 minutes)

1. Ask volunteers to read the information about the organization of an outline.
2. Check comprehension: *Why might you use an outline? What is one way to organize it? What should you include in an outline.*

web For additional practice with using an outline, have students visit *Q Online Practice.*

DETAILS (10 minutes)

A (10 minutes)

1. Have students complete the activity individually.
2. Have students compare answers with a partner. Then elicit the answers from volunteers.

Details A Answers, p. 164

1. Thesis statement: …many recent graduates say that they struggle with the transition from classroom to career world and have difficulty adjusting to life on the job.

2. Main idea: Lewis believes that most of our school experiences—from childhood through university—are fairly predictable, while life in the working world is far more ambiguous.

Supporting ideas:

In school, for example, the pattern stays more or less the same from year to year. All students have to take….

In the workplace, however, constant change is the norm, and one has to adapt quickly. A project you are working on….

Lewis notes that in school, for example, you advance each year to the next grade….

In the workplace, however, "you have no idea when you might be promoted; it depends on the economy,…."

▶ *Reading and Writing 4, page 164*

B (15 minutes)

1. Direct students to complete the outline. Remind them to look at Activity A as an example.
2. Elicit answers from volunteers. You may want to project the page to fill in the answers.

Details B Answers, p. 164

III. Recent graduates are not prepared to think analytically.
A. In school, students memorize facts and take tests.
B. In the workplace, they must think critically and make decisions.
C. Schools should spend less time on testing.
D. Schools should spend more time on helping students analyze information, solve problems, and communicate ideas.

IV. Many recent graduates have difficulty adjusting to teamwork.
A. In school, students work independently and get grades based on how they have done.
B. In the workplace, we are often dependent on co-workers for our success.

V. Ways we can better prepare students for the workplace
A. All students should do an internship.
B. Include more teamwork as part of class activities.
C. There should be more focus on developing writing and public speaking skills.

web For additional practice with reading comprehension, have students visit *Q Online Practice*.

Tip for Success (1 minute)

Ask a volunteer to read the tip aloud. Then explain: *It's important to manage your time well. Reading an outline allows you to quickly review the important points.*

Reading and Writing 4, page 165

WHAT DO YOU THINK? (20 minutes)

1. Ask students to read the questions and reflect on their answers.
2. Seat students in small groups and assign roles: a group leader to make sure everyone contributes, a note-taker to record the group's ideas, a reporter to share the group's ideas with the class, and a timekeeper to watch the clock. Give students five minutes to discuss the questions. Then call on each group's reporter to share ideas with the class.
3. Have each student choose one of the questions and write for 5–10 minutes in response.
4. Call on volunteers to share their responses.

MULTILEVEL OPTION:

Pair lower-level students and have them choose the same question to respond to.

As higher-level students finish writing, have them share their responses with a partner.

What Do You Think? Activity Answers, p. 165

Answers will vary. Sample answers:

1. I think doing an internship while you are in school is a great idea because students learn practical skills for their future jobs.
2. Schools should prepare students to effectively use technology. Many jobs require employees to use company email, navigate the Internet, or make PowerPoint presentations. These skills should be taught in schools.
3. On a scale of 1 to 5, I would give my school a 2 for how well it prepared me for work. I didn't have many opportunities to work in a group, which I have to do at work all the time. Also, I wish I'd had more training with computers before I got my job.

Critical Thinking Tip (3 minutes)

1. Ask a volunteer to read the tip aloud.
2. Elicit ideas from students about how they justify their opinions. Their answers may include recalling information from texts or experience, analyzing that information to see if it's logical, and making changes based on this analysis.

Critical Q: Expansion Activity

Justify Your Opinions in a Debate

Have students practice justifying their opinions and giving reasons by staging a debate based on Question #1 on p. 165.

Put students into three groups and assign each group one suggestion from Reading 1 (internships, more teamwork, or focus on writing/public speaking skills). Each group should analyze the suggestion and brainstorm reasons to support it.

Have representatives from each group debate why their suggestion is important and point out why it is better than the others.

Learning Outcome

Use the Learning Outcome to frame the purpose and relevance of Reading 1. Ask: *What did you learn from Reading 1 that prepares you to summarize and paraphrase the author's purpose, thesis, main ideas, and conclusions?* (Students learned how a text is organized through using an outline. This skill can help them when they summarize a text for their Unit Assignment.)

READING 2:
Making My First Post-College Decision

VOCABULARY (15 minutes)

1. Have students read the words and the definitions. Answer questions about meaning and provide examples of the words in context.
2. Direct students to complete the sentences with the vocabulary words. Then call on volunteers to read the sentences aloud.

Vocabulary Answers, pp. 165–166

1. income; **2.** incentive; **3.** contact;
4. enable; **5.** particular; **6.** reluctant;
7. permanent; **8.** utilize; **9.** approach;
10. institution; **11.** acquire

web For additional practice with the vocabulary, have students visit *Q Online Practice*.

Reading and Writing 4, page 166

PREVIEW READING 2 (10 minutes)

1. Read the introduction. Discuss what a blog is. Remind students about skimming a text.
2. Tell students to skim (not read) the first paragraph and answer the questions. After two minutes, elicit answers from volunteers.
3. Tell students to review their answers after reading.

Preview Reading 2 Answers, p. 166

1. He's trying to decide between starting his own business (working for himself) or taking a job in a large corporation.
2. Answers will vary.

Reading and Writing 4, page 167

Reading 2 Background Note

Entrepreneurs are creative, independent individuals who take advantage of new opportunities. Often they take financial risks to start a new company or project.

Vera Wang is a successful entrepreneur. Inspired by her frustrating search for the perfect wedding gown, Wang started her own bridal gown shop. Her dresses are known for their simple designs and rich fabrics. Today, her company is a multi-million dollar success.

Ray Kroc, founder of McDonald's, is another example of a successful entrepreneur. He once said, "The two most important requirements for major success are: first, being in the right place at the right time, and second, doing something about it." Kroc expanded a small California hamburger restaurant into a successful worldwide chain.

READ (20 minutes)

CD2 Track 7

1. Have students read the blog entry. Remind them to refer to the glossed words as they read.
2. When students have finished reading, answer any questions about vocabulary. Then play the audio and have students follow along.

Reading and Writing 4, page 169

MAIN IDEAS

A (10 minutes)

1. Have students read the headings first. Then have them identify the main idea of each paragraph and match it to the best heading. Remind them that one of the headings will not be used.
2. Elicit the answers from volunteers.

Main Ideas A Answers, p. 169

a. 5; **b.** 3; **c.** 6; **d.** not used;
e. 2; **f.** 7; **g.** 1; **h.** 4

B (10 minutes)

Have partners complete the activity together. Then call on pairs to share their answers.

Main Ideas B Answers, p. 169

Answers will vary.

DETAILS (10 minutes)

1. Direct students to mark the statements *T* or *F* and to correct the false statements.
2. Have students compare answers with a partner and go back to the article to check their answers. Then go over the answers with the class.

Details Answers, p. 169

1. F (The blogger *isn't* interested in a career in telecommunications.);
2. T;
3. F (He plans to start working full time in *July after* he graduates.);
4. F (He believes that *accounting* firms pay higher salaries than *telecommunication* firms.);
5. T;
6. T;
7. F (Having *job flexibility or choices* is the writer's goal.);
8. T

For additional practice with reading comprehension, have students visit *Q Online Practice*.

Reading and Writing 4, page 170

WHAT DO YOU THINK?

A (15 minutes)

1. Ask students to read the questions and reflect on their answers.
2. Seat students in small groups and assign roles: a group leader to make sure everyone contributes, a note-taker to record the group's ideas, a reporter to share the group's ideas with the class, and a timekeeper to watch the clock.
3. Give students five minutes to discuss the questions. Call time if conversations are winding down. Allow them an extra minute or two if necessary.
4. Then have students choose one of the questions and write a paragraph in response.
5. Call on volunteers to share their responses.

What Do You Think? Activity A Answers, p. 170

Answers will vary. Sample answers:

1. I think the blogger has made good career choices. I admire him for taking a position that would get him experience in his field and help him to continue learning new things.
2. One of my career goals is to become a nurse. To do this, I need to finish nursing school and pass my exams by next year.

B (10 minutes)

1. Tell students that they should think about both Reading 1 and Reading 2 as they discuss the questions in Activity B.
2. Ask each group's reporter to share the group's answers with the class.

What Do You Think? Activity B Answers, p. 170

Answers will vary. Sample answers:

1. I think a person should get a part-time job or travel to get some life experience before beginning a future career.
2. An advantage of this attitude is that you can work at a few different jobs to see what you like best. A disadvantage is that you may find it difficult to get a permanent job in the future.

Learning Outcome

Use the Learning Outcome to frame the purpose and relevance of Readings 1 and 2. Ask: *What did you learn from Readings 1 and 2 that prepares you to summarize and paraphrase the author's purpose, thesis, main ideas, and conclusions?* (Students read two different views about getting a job after school.)

Vocabulary Skill: Word Forms (10 minutes)

1. Call on students to read the information about word forms. Check comprehension: *What are word forms? How will this skill help you with writing and speaking?*
2. Provide another word, such as *environment,* and show students how to use the dictionary to find the word forms *(environmentalist; environmental; environmentally).*

Skill Note

Help students identify word forms by teaching common suffixes that indicate a word's part of speech. For example, words that end with *-er, –tion,* or *-sion* are nouns. Words that end with *-ence* or *-ance* also tend to be nouns. Some suffixes that indicate that a word is in adjective are *-ent, –ant,* and *-ful.* Some suffixes commonly found in verbs are *–ate* and *–ize.* By teaching students to recognize these common suffixes, they will more easily be able to identify different word forms of a new word.

Reading and Writing 4, page 171

A (15 minutes)

1. Direct students to work in pairs and use a dictionary to complete the activity.
2. Go over the answers with the class.

Vocabulary Skill A Answers, p. 171

1. acquire, acquisition;
2. adjust, adjustment, adjustable;
3. ambiguity, ambiguous, ambiguously;
4. anticipate, anticipation, anticipated;
5. collaborate, collaboration, collaborative, collaboratively;
6. constant, constant, constantly;
7. interpret, interpretation, interpretive;
8. particulars, particular, particularly;
9. permanence, permanent, permanently;
10. reluctance, reluctant, reluctantly

Tip for Success (5 minutes)

Read the tip aloud. Then review the differences in pronunciation based on the word forms: *acquire* vs. *acquisition; ambiguity* vs. *ambiguous/ambiguously; anticipate(d)* vs. *anticipation; collaborate/collaborative(ly)* vs. *collaboration; interpret/interpretive* vs. *interpretation.*

B (15 minutes)

1. Direct students to complete the sentences and then compare their answers with a partner.
2. Call on volunteers to read the sentences.

Vocabulary Skill B Answers, pp. 171–172

1a. adjustment;	**1b.** adjustable;
2a. constantly;	**2b.** constant;
3a. permanently;	**3b.** permanent;
4a. reluctant;	**4b.** reluctantly;
5a. ambiguous;	**5b.** ambiguously;
6a. collaborate;	**6b.** collaboration;
7a. anticipated;	**7b.** anticipate;
8a. particulars;	**8b.** particularly

▶ *Reading and Writing 4, page 172*

C (10 minutes)

1. Direct students to write their sentences. Then have them read their sentences to a partner.
2. Ask volunteers to write their sentences on the board. Correct any errors with the word forms. Point out any changes in pronunciation.

Vocabulary Skill C Answers, p. 172

Answers will vary. Sample answers:

1. I want to collaborate with you on this project. / This project was a collaboration between sales and marketing. / Our project was a collaborative effort from two different departments.
2. The students feel some reluctance to apply for jobs in a different field. / The worker is reluctant to ask for a raise. / She reluctantly entered her boss's office to discuss the problem.

web For an additional practice with word forms, have students visit *Q Online Practice.*

▶ *Reading and Writing 4, page 173*

WRITING

Writing Skill: Writing a summary (10 minutes)

1. Read the information about writing a summary.
2. Check comprehension: *What is a summary? What should you do before you write a summary? What should you include in your summary? Do you use the author's words or your own words in a summary?*

Tip for Success (1 minute)

Ask a volunteer to read the tip aloud. Then explain: *An outline is a kind of summary. Making an outline helps you to pull out key information from a text. A good outline will help you to write a clear, thorough summary.*

A (15 minutes)

1. Direct students to complete the activity. Remind them to follow the directions carefully.
2. Have students share their answers with a partner before discussing them as a class.

Writing Skill A Answers, p. 174

1. c
2. Thesis statement: …there are some simple ways to prepare for a job interview.
3. Main ideas: Make a list of questions you might be asked at the interview. Think about possible answers to the questions and practice responding to them.
4. b

Reading and Writing 4, page 175

B (10 minutes)

1. Direct students to read the summaries, complete the checklist, and answer the questions.
2. Discuss the answers as a class.

Writing Skill B Answers, p. 175

Summary 1: Sentences 1-8 should be checked.
Summary 2: Sentences 3, 4, and 7 should be checked.

1. Summary 1 is better.
2. Answers will vary. Possible answers: Summary 1 is better than Summary 2 because it gives more information and all of the information is correct. / Summary 1 is better because it is clear and easy to follow.

For additional practice with writing a summary, have students visit *Q Online Practice*.

21ST CENTURY SKILLS

It is important for students to be able to identify the most important ideas in a text and present them in a clear, organized way. In the workplace, students may be required to summarize information by presenting key points from a meeting, conference, or presentation or by briefing a supervisor on the progress of a day's work. Ask students to brainstorm other ways that they may use summarizing in their jobs.

Reading and Writing 4, page 176

Grammar: Reported speech with the present tense (15 minutes)

1. Ask volunteers to read each section about reported speech. Highlight the examples and provide additional ones to reinforce the skill.
2. Check comprehension: *Why is present tense used with reported speech in academic writing? What types of clauses are used in reported speech?*

Skill Note

In academic writing, opinions and research are reported in the present tense. Unlike conversation, where *say* and *tell* are used almost exclusively, academic writing uses a wider range of verbs.

Some additional reporting verbs that are used in academic writing are *mentions, notes, claims, concludes, recommends,* and *stresses.*

Tip for Success (1 minute)

Ask a volunteer to read the tip aloud. Then explain: *The reporting clause may not always identify a single person's words or ideas. Sometimes the subject will be general, such as "Many people believe…."*

Reading and Writing 4, page 177

A (10 minutes)

Direct students to complete the activity and compare their answers with a partner. Then call on volunteers to share their answers.

Grammar A Answers, p. 177

1. Reporting clause: many recent graduates say; Noun clause: that they have difficulty adjusting to life on the job
2. Reporting clause: Joseph Lewis notes; Noun clause: that in school, you advance each year, but at work the same isn't true
3. Does not use reported speech
4. Reporting clause: Many people wonder; Noun clause: how we can better prepare young adults for the workplace
5. Reporting clause: One recent report tells educators; Noun clause: that less time should be spent on testing in school
6. Reporting clause: recent graduates explain; Noun clause: what current students can do to prepare
7. Does not use reported speech
8. Reporting clause: Other graduates feel; Noun clause: there should be more focus on developing writing and public speaking skills

B (5 minutes)

1. Direct students to circle the best answer.
2. Go over the answers with the class.

Grammar B Answers, p. 177

1. a; **2.** c; **3.** b; **4.** c; **5.** c; **6.** c

For additional practice with reported speech with the present tense, have students visit *Q Online Practice*.

Reading and Writing 4, page 178

C (15 minutes)

1. Have students complete the activity and then compare sentences with a partner.
2. Ask volunteers to write the sentences on the board. Correct them as a class. Discuss the changes in pronouns in sentences 1, 4, 5, and 6.

Grammar C Answers, p. 178

2. The news article says (that) many recent graduates aren't ready for the workplace.
3. Many students believe (that) learning a second language is challenging.
4. Tara wonders how she can get a good job.
5. Many students want to know what they should do after graduation.
6. The school handbook tells students which courses they must take to graduate. / The school handbook tells students (that) they must take four years of English and three years of math to graduate.

Unit Assignment: Write a summary

Unit Question (5 minutes)

Refer students back to the ideas they discussed at the beginning of the unit about how school prepares them for work. Cue students by asking specific questions about the content of the unit: *What skills did you learn in school? Do these skills help you in your job? Does the author of Reading 1 feel that school prepares students for work?*

Learning Outcome

1. Tie the Unit Assignment to the unit Learning Outcome. Say: *The outcome for this unit is to write a summary. This Unit Assignment is going to let you show your skill at writing a summary paragraph as well as using reported speech.*
2. Explain that you are going to use a rubric similar to their Self-Assessment checklist on p. 180 to grade their Unit Assignment. You can also share a copy of the Unit Assignment Rubric (on p. 77 of this *Teacher's Handbook*) with the students.

Reading and Writing 4, page 179

Plan and Write

Brainstorm

A (15 minutes)

Help students with reevaluating their outline on page 164. Remind them of how helpful it can be to write an outline before writing a summary.

Plan

B (15 minutes)

Tell students to use the information in the outline from page 164 to help them plan their summary.

Tip for Success (1 minute)

1. Ask a volunteer to read the tip aloud.
2. Explain: *When you want to include another person's ideas in your writing, it's important that you give them credit by including their name. If you don't, you may accidentally plagiarize.*

Reading and Writing 4, page 180

Write

C (20 minutes)

1. Direct students to look at the Self-Assessment checklist before they begin writing.
2. Circulate around the room to answer students' questions and guide them as they write.

Tip for Success (1 minute)

Read the tip aloud. Then explain: *When you use reported speech in your writing, you can change it to fit your needs. You can make it longer or shorter. You may also want to explain some key ideas more so your readers understand the full context of the person's words.*

Alternative Unit Assignments

Assign or have students choose one of these assignments to do instead of, or in addition to, the Unit Assignment.

1. Write a summary of "Making My First Post-College Career Decision."
2. Write 1–2 paragraphs discussing two possible career paths you are considering, such as working in a large company or having your own business. Discuss the skills you need and the advantages of each career path. Use the information in the readings to support your ideas.

For an additional Unit Assignment, have students visit *Q Online Practice*.

Revise and Edit

Peer Review

A (15 minutes)

1. Pair students and direct them to read each other's work.
2. Ask students to answer and discuss the questions.
3. Give students suggestions of helpful feedback: *Remember to state the author's purpose. I like the way you used the author's words in reported speech. Don't forget to add the main idea of the second paragraph.*

Rewrite

B (10 minutes)

Students should review their partners' answers from A and rewrite their paragraphs if necessary.

Edit

C (10 minutes)

1. Direct students to read and complete the Self-Assessment checklist. They should be prepared to hand in their work or discuss it in class.
2. Ask for a show of hands for how many students gave all or mostly *yes* answers.
3. Use the Unit Assignment Rubric on p. 77 in this *Teacher's Handbook* to score each student's assignment.
4. Alternatively, divide the class into large groups and have students read their summaries to their group. Pass out copies of the Unit Assignment Rubric and have students grade each other.

▶ *Reading and Writing 4, page 181*

Track Your Success (5 minutes)

1. Have students circle the words they have learned in this unit. Suggest that students go back through the unit to review any words they have forgotten.
2. Have students check the skills they have mastered. If students need more practice to feel confident about their proficiency in a skill, point out the page numbers and encourage them to review.
3. Read the Learning Outcome aloud. Ask students if they feel that they have met the outcome.

Unit Assignment Rubric

Student name: ______________________________

Date: __________

Unit Assignment: *Write a summary.*

20 points = Summary element was completely successful (at least 90% of the time).
15 points = Summary element was mostly successful (at least 70% of the time).
10 points = Summary element was partially successful (at least 50% of the time).
0 points = Summary element was not successful.

Write a Summary	20 points	15 points	10 points	0 points
Summary includes the title of the article and the author's name and purpose.				
Summary identifies the thesis statement and includes all the main ideas of the article.				
Summary is written mostly in the student's own words.				
Reported speech is used correctly.				
Punctuation, spelling, and grammar are correct.				

Total points: __________

Comments:

UNIT 8

Unit QUESTION
Is discovery always a good thing?

Discovery

READING • understanding the purpose of quoted speech
VOCABULARY • word roots
WRITING • writing an opinion essay
GRAMMAR • adverb phrases of reason

LEARNING OUTCOME

Defend your opinion about whether a specific discovery or type of exploration is a good or bad thing.

Reading and Writing 4, pages 182–183

Preview the Unit

Learning Outcome

1. Ask for a volunteer to read the unit skills and the unit Learning Outcome.
2. Explain: *This is what you are expected to be able to do by the unit's end. The Learning Outcome explains how you are going to be evaluated. With this outcome in mind, you should focus on learning those skills (Reading, Vocabulary, Writing, Grammar) that will support your goal of defending your opinion about whether a discovery or exploration is good or bad. This can also help you act as mentors in the classroom to help other students meet this Learning Outcome.*

A (15 minutes)

1. Ask students: *What does it mean to "discover" something? How is this different from finding something that is lost (like your keys)?*
2. Have pairs to discuss the first two questions.
3. Call on volunteers to share their ideas. List some of the discoveries on the board. Ask: *Which of these discoveries is exciting to you? Is it OK to spend a lot of money to make new discoveries?*
4. Focus students' attention on the photo. Have a volunteer describe the photo to the class. Read the third question aloud. Elicit students' answers.

Preview the Unit A Answers, p. 183

Answers will vary. Sample answers:

1. Scientists recently discovered a way to clone cows. That's exciting because there are hungry people in the world who could eat meat from these cows.
2. It's important to spend money on exploration, especially in the fields of science or medicine.
3. This is Machu Picchu. Tourists are visiting the site.

B (10 minutes)

1. Introduce the Unit Question: "Is discovery always a good thing?" Ask related information questions or questions about personal experience to help students prepare for answering the more abstract Unit Question. For example, ask: *What are some places that people explore? What are they looking for?*
2. Read the Unit question aloud. Give students a minute to silently consider their answers to the question. Say: *Let's consider discoveries. What are the advantages of discoveries? What are the disadvantages?*
3. Write *Discoveries* at the top of two sheets of poster paper with the sub-categories *Advantages* and *Disadvantages.*
4. Elicit students' answers and write them in the correct categories. Post the lists to refer to later in the unit.

Preview the Unit B Answers, p. 183

Answers will vary. Sample answers:

Lower-level answer: Yes, because we might find a cure for a disease, like cancer.

On-level answer: I don't think that discoveries are always good. For example, someone discovered how to make a hydrogen bomb, and it was used to kill people.

Higher-level answer: In my opinion, there are advantages and disadvantages to every discovery. One advantage of discovering oil in the sea is that we can use it for energy. But sometimes there are oil spills, so there are disadvantages to this discovery as well.

The Q Classroom (5 minutes)

CD2 Track 8

1. Play *The Q Classroom*. Use the example from the audio to help students continue the conversation. Ask: *How did the students answer the question? Do you agree or disagree with their ideas? Why?*

2. Ask students to write 2-3 sentences explaining their current opinion. Tell them they should look back on their opinion at the end of the unit.

Reading and Writing 4, page 184

C (10 minutes)

1. Direct students to read the information about each person. Then have students talk with a partner about which person they think is doing the most important work and why.
2. Elicit opinions from volunteers.

MULTILEVEL OPTION

Have higher-level students write a short paragraph in response to the people and discoveries they read about in Activity C. They should discuss which person is making the most interesting or important discoveries for society.

Preview the Unit C Answers, p. 184
Answers will vary. Sample answer:
Will Steger is doing the most important work because he is studying the effects of global warming in the Arctic. This will help us learn more about what we need to do to prevent flooding and other natural disasters.

D (15 minutes)

1. Read the directions aloud. Put students into small groups and direct them to discuss the questions.
2. Remind students that their decision must be unanimous, meaning everyone must agree.

Preview the Unit D Answers, p. 184
Answers will vary. Sample answers:

1. Yes, Will Steger's work helps everyone on our planet.
2. "Zeray" Alemseged's discovery of the oldest known skeleton of a human helps us to better understand the history of humans on our planet.
3. Yes, Constance Adam's design of an international space station for the first human mission to Mars will help future generations study and explore other planets in space.
4. An award of $500,000 would help Robert Ballard continue to improve his design of machines for deep-sea exploration.

E (5 minutes)

Call on each group to announce their decision and give reasons for their selection.

Preview the Unit E Answers, p. 183
Answers will vary.

EXPANSION ACTIVITY: Debate (20 minutes)

1. Organize a debate about who should receive the prize money. Put students into four groups and assign them a discoverer from Activity C.
2. Have groups brainstorm the merits of their discoverer and why he/she deserves the prize money (based on the criteria in Activity D).
3. Have representatives from each group argue their case to the class. After each group's argument, encourage other groups to respond.
4. Choose a group of students to be the "judge" or invite another instructor to judge the debate. The judge should choose the winning group based on their arguments.

READING

Reading and Writing 4, page 185

READING 1: A Tribe is Discovered

VOCABULARY (15 minutes)

1. Direct students' attention to the picture. Ask: *Do you know anything about the Yeti?*
2. Ask volunteers to read the excerpt aloud.
3. Direct students to write each bold word next to the correct definition. Remind them to use context clues in the excerpt to help them.

MULTILEVEL OPTION

Pair lower-level students and provide them with sample sentences using the vocabulary words. For example, *I can't confirm if I will attend the meeting because I may have class at that time. The two children had a conflict over the ball. They both wanted to play with it.*

Have higher-level students write an additional sentence for each vocabulary word. Ask volunteers to write their sentences on the board. Correct the sentences, focusing on the meaning and use of the words rather than other grammatical issues.

Vocabulary Answers, pp. 185–186

1. inevitable;	**2.** deter;	**3.** motives;
4. cite;	**5.** moral;	**6.** dilemma;
7. genuinely;	**8.** adopt;	**9.** confirm;
10. fatal;	**11.** hostile;	**12.** conflict

web For additional practice with the vocabulary, have students visit *Q Online Practice.*

Reading and Writing 4, page 186

PREVIEW READING 1 (10 minutes)

1. Direct students to read the introduction and answer the question. Then have students discuss their answer with a partner.
2. Tell students to review their answer after reading.

Preview Reading 1 Answer, p. 186

Answers will vary. Sample answer:
I imagine the tribe was very surprised and afraid.

Reading 1 Background Note

Technology makes us feel like the world is smaller than ever. We can communicate with others across the globe in seconds, yet there are still some places in our modern world that remain extremely isolated.

The Pitcairn Islands are a group of four small volcanic islands in the southern Pacific Ocean. Its population is estimated to be about 50 people. Access to the islands is difficult due to steep cliffs and pounding waves.

Alert, a small village on the Arctic Ocean in Canada, has only five year-round inhabitants. Its extreme weather and months of complete sunlight or darkness make it a challenging place to live. The nearest town is a fishing village 1,300 miles (2,092 kilometers) away.

READ (20 minutes)

CD2, Track 9

1. Instruct students to read the article.
2. When students have finished reading, answer any questions they may have about the article or additional vocabulary. Then play the audio and have students follow along.

Reading and Writing 4, page 188

MAIN IDEAS (15 minutes)

Have students answer the questions and compare their answers with a partner. Then elicit the answers from volunteers.

Main Ideas Answers, p. 188

1. The purpose was to show that the tribe exists.
2. The moral dilemma is whether to make contact or leave them alone.
3. Fifty percent of them died. Some were shot and some died by disease.
4. Hill recommends leaving the tribe alone and not making further contact.
5. Dr. Bourque thinks they need to be contacted by appropriate people with good motives.

Reading and Writing 4, page 189

DETAILS (10 minutes)

1. Direct students to circle the best answers.
2. Have students compare answers with a partner.
3. Go over the answers with the class.

Details Answers, p. 189

1. b; **2.** c; **3.** a; **4.** a; **5.** b; **6.** c; **7.** c

For additional practice with reading comprehension, have students visit *Q Online Practice*.

Reading and Writing 4, page 190

WHAT DO YOU THINK? (20 minutes)

1. Ask students to read the questions and reflect on their answers.
2. Seat students in small groups and assign roles: a group leader to make sure everyone contributes, a note-taker to record the group's ideas, a reporter to share the group's ideas with the class, and a timekeeper to watch the clock. Give students five minutes to discuss the questions.
3. Call on each group's reporter to share ideas with the class.
4. Have each student choose one of the questions and write for 5–10 minutes in response.
5. Call on volunteers to share their responses.

MULTILEVEL OPTION:

Have lower-level students work in pairs to write a response to the same question while higher-level students work individually. Call on pairs or individuals to share their responses with the class.

What Do You Think? Activity Answers, p. 190

Answers will vary. Sample answers:

1. I don't think the authorities should contact the Acre tribe. They have been there for a long time and should be left alone.
2. Some benefits of the modern world that could help the tribe are modern medicine and machines. Some risks would be that the tribe might not adjust to modern life, which could have an impact on their health.
3. Tourists should not be allowed to visit tribes like the Acre. It is unethical to interfere with their lives simply for entertainment.

Learning Outcome

Use the Learning Outcome to frame the purpose and relevance of Reading 1. Ask: *What did you learn from Reading 1 that prepares you to defend your opinion about whether a discovery or exploration is a good or bad thing?* (Students learned about recent discoveries of people who live in extreme isolation and how contact with the modern world has negatively impacted their lives.)

Reading Skill: Understanding the purpose of quoted speech (10 minutes)

1. Ask a volunteer to read about the purpose of quoted speech. Review the differences between facts and opinions.
2. Check comprehension: *When might you use a quotation?*

Tip for Success (1 minute)

Read the tip aloud. Then explain: *Pay attention to who a writer quotes. The writer may or may not agree with the opinions he or she quotes.*

A (5 minutes)

1. Direct students to find the quotations in the reading and label them *NB* or *DH*.
2. Have students compare the labels with a partner. Elicit the quotations from volunteers. You may want to project the reading to show the labeling.

Reading Skill A Answers, p. 190

Dr. Nicole Bourque (NB):
Para 7: "Some will say leave them untouched. Others, probably the majority, will say . . . At least then the first outsiders they meet are decent people."
Para 16: "You get the curiosity factor, and you want your picture taken . . . People do not think about the long-term impact on these communities."
Para 18: "It would be better if first contact came from . . . who could prepare them for the future and what might happen."
David Hill (DH):
Para 10: "They were forcibly contacted by illegal loggers . . . but most died from diseases that were introduced to them."
Para 12: "What has happened is they have moved even deeper into the forest."
Para 13: "It puts pressure on governments to stop the logging. I have no doubt that. . . If you don't know where they are, then you can't protect them as well."
Para 14: "We would warn strongly against further contact."

B (5 minutes)

Have students answer the question by reviewing the quotes from the article.

Reading Skill B Answer, p. 190

Nicole Bourque

C (10 minutes)

1. Direct students to label each quotation *F* or *O*.
2. Elicit answers from students. Discuss the language in each sentence that makes it a fact or an opinion.

Reading Skill C Answers, pp. 190–191

1. F; **2.** O; **3.** F; **4.** F;
5. O; **6.** F; **7.** F; **8.** O

web For additional practice with understanding the purpose of quoted speech, have students visit *Q Online Practice*.

Reading and Writing 4, page 191

READING 2: The Kipunji

VOCABULARY (15 minutes)

1. Have students read the vocabulary words and their definitions. Answer any questions about meaning. Model the pronunciation of the words.
2. Direct students to complete each sentence with the correct vocabulary word.
3. Call on volunteers to read the sentences.

Vocabulary Answers, pp. 191–192

1. conversion; **2.** restricted; **3.** multiple;
4. species; **5.** critically; **6.** extinction;
7. restoration; **8.** range; **9.** conservation;
10. specimen; **11.** habitat; **12.** classify

web For additional practice with the vocabulary, have students visit *Q Online Practice*.

Reading and Writing 4, page 192

PREVIEW READING 2 (5 minutes)

1. Read the introduction. Have students think about their answer before discussing it with a partner.
2. Tell students to review their answer after reading.

Preview Reading 2 Answer, p. 192

Answers will vary. Sample answer:
Newly discovered animals might face dangers from humans. Humans may accidentally harm the animal and its habitat.

Reading 2 Background Note

In biology, extinction means the end of an organism. The Dodo bird is a famously extinct animal, last seen in the late 1600s. It was killed off by humans who destroyed the forests where it lived. Some common causes of extinction are habitat destruction, predators, and disease. According to the World Wildlife Fund (WWF), the destructive activities of humans have caused the rate of species extinction to be 100 to 1,000 times greater than its natural rate.

READ (20 minutes)

CD2, Track 10

1. Instruct students to read the article. Remind them to refer to the glossed words as they read.
2. When students have finished reading, answer any questions they may have about the article. Then play the audio and have students follow along.

Reading and Writing 4, page 195

MAIN IDEAS (10 minutes)

1. Direct students to mark each statement *T* or *F* and correct the false statements. Then have them compare answers with a partner.
2. Elicit the answers from volunteers.

Main Ideas Answers, p. 195

1. T;
2. T;
3. T;
4. F (The kipunji live in two isolated areas.);
5. F (The WCS thinks the kipunji should be classified as critically endangered.);
6. F (The WCS is working to protect and restore kipunji habitat.)

DETAILS (10 minutes)

1. Direct students to complete each sentence. Then have them compare answers with a partner.
2. Go over the answers with the class.

Details Answers, p. 195

1. genus;
2. its home on Mt. Rungwe
3. a farmer;
4. the baboon/baboons;
5. Wildlife Conservation Society;
6. 1,117;
7. (illegal) logging; land conversion; poachers;
8. 1923

For additional practice with reading comprehension, have students visit *Q Online Practice*.

Reading and Writing 4, page 196

WHAT DO YOU THINK?

A (15 minutes)

1. Ask students to read the questions and reflect on their answers.
2. Seat students in small groups and assign roles: a group leader to make sure everyone contributes, a note-taker to record the group's ideas, a reporter to share the group's ideas with the class, and a timekeeper to watch the clock. Give students five minutes to discuss the questions.
3. Have each student choose one of the questions and write a paragraph in response.
4. Call on volunteers to share their responses.

What Do You Think? Activity A Answers, p. 196

Answers will vary. Sample answers:

1. I think being discovered was good for the kipunji because they were headed toward extinction anyway. People know they are a rare species, so their habitat will be preserved.
2. I think the white rhino is an endangered species. Scientists are breeding them in zoos to try to prevent them from becoming extinct.

B (10 minutes)

1. Tell the students that they should think about both Reading 1 and Reading 2 as they discuss the questions in Activity B.
2. Call on each group's reporter to give a brief summary of their group's discussion.

What Do You Think? Activity B Answers, p. 196

Answers will vary. Sample answers:

1. I disagree that all the major discoveries have been made. How can we really know? Maybe we will look back on this time in 200 years and think of how little we knew.
2. I understand why we want to explore the last wild places, but I don't think it's right. We should allow nature to exist peacefully without interfering with it.

Critical Thinking Tip (1 minute)

1. Ask a volunteer to read the tip aloud.
2. Explain: *We usually base our ideas and opinions on information from different sources, such as books or articles we've read or our own experiences.*

Learning Outcome

Use the Learning Outcome to frame the purpose and relevance of Readings 1 and 2. Ask: *What did you learn from Readings 1 and 2 that prepares you to defend your opinion about whether a discovery or exploration is good or bad?* (Students learned about the discoveries of people and animals that had not been seen or studied before. These ideas may help them when they plan their Unit Assignment.)

Vocabulary Skill: Word roots (10 minutes)

1. Call on volunteers to read the information aloud.
2. Check comprehension: *What language do many words come from? What is a word root? Why is it useful to know the basic meaning of word roots?*

Skill Note

Word roots are clues to the meaning of words. Knowing word roots can help students figure out the meaning of new words. In addition to the ones on p. 197, here are some other common word roots.

The root *-act-* means "to do" or "to move" and forms words such as *action*, *react*, and *activity*.

The root *-cred-* means "to believe" and forms words like *incredible*, *credit*, and *credential*.

The root *-log-* means "word" or "speech" and forms words such as *dialog*, *apology*, and *logic*.

▶ ***Reading and Writing 4, page 197***

A (10 minutes)

1. Have partners complete the activity together.
2. Elicit the answers from volunteers.

Vocabulary Skill A Answers, p. 197

Other examples:	Basic meaning:
2. generate, genus;	**2.** produce;
3. portable, transport;	**3.** carry;
4. conscious, unconscious;	**4.** know;
5. inscribe, manuscript;	**5.** write;
6. inspect, speculate;	**6.** look;
7. reverse, versatile;	**7.** turn;
8. video, vision	**8.** see

B (15 minutes)

1. Direct students to complete the activity individually and then read their sentences to a partner. Encourage them to use their dictionaries if they need help.
2. Have students write their sentences on the board.

Vocabulary Skill B Answers, p. 197

Answers will vary. Sample sentences:

2. I try to be **conscious** of how my actions affect other people.
3. His ideas about global warming **generated** a passionate discussion.
4. The policeman **inspected** the crime scene.
5. My wedding date is **inscribed** on my ring.
6. She likes to buy **versatile** clothes that she can wear to work and on the weekends.

web+ For additional practice with word roots, have students visit *Q Online Practice*.

▶ ***Reading and Writing 4, page 198***

WRITING

Writing Skill: Writing an opinion essay (5 minutes)

Read the about writing an opinion essay to students. Then check comprehension: *What is the purpose of an opinion essay? What do you express in the introduction? What should you include in the body paragraphs?*

A (15 minutes)

1. Direct students to read the essay and complete the activity.
2. Have students compare their answers with a partner. Then discuss the answers as a class.

Writing Skill A Answers, p. 198

Thesis statement: We must continue to invest in exploration of the deep sea so that we can take advantage of its benefits.

Main reasons:

Paragraph 1: The deep seas contain resources that could bring improvements in the field of medicine.

Paragraph 2: At a time when existing forms of fuel are limited, the deep ocean could provide new sources of fuel.

Paragraph 3: Finally, using the deep sea for the disposal of nuclear waste is a controversial issue that needs to be explored further.

▶ ***Reading and Writing 4, page 199***

Tip for Success (1 minute)

Read the tip aloud. Then explain: *The purpose of writing an outline is to save time and summarize key ideas, so you should not copy entire sentences from the text.*

B (15 minutes)

1. Have students work with a partner to complete the outline.
2. Elicit the missing information from volunteers. You may want to copy the outline on the board.

Writing Skill B Answers, p. 199

I. Thesis statement: We need to invest in exploration of the ocean in order to take advantage of its benefits.

II. Reason 1: The deep seas could bring improvements in medicine.
A. Support 1: Plant life in the deep ocean may lead to new medicines.
B. Support 2: Scientists who researched this area won a Nobel Prize.

III. Reason 2: The deep ocean could provide new sources of fuel.
A. Support 1: There is a lot of oil beneath the ocean bed.
B. Support 2: Methane in the ocean is a possible source of fuel.

IV. Reason 3: The ocean may be a solution to the problem of nuclear waste.
A. Support 1: Waste could be sealed into the ocean floor.
B. Support 2: Ocean disposal could be safer than current methods.

V. Concluding idea: Advances in our knowledge justify the expense of deep-sea exploration.

web For additional practice with writing an opinion essay, have students visit *Q Online Practice*.

Critical Q: Expansion Activity

Evaluate Reasons and Support

Activity B on pp. 198–199 asks students to read an opinion essay and outline the author's ideas.

As students identify each reason (e.g. *The deep sea could bring improvements in medicine*), have them evaluate it based on the author's supporting details (e.g. *Plant life in the ocean may lead to new medicines*). Ask: *Do the details the author gives convince you that this is a valid reason? In your opinion, which of the two supporting details is more effective?*

Have students discuss their ideas in pairs.

21ST CENTURY SKILLS

In the workplace, employees may be asked to express their opinions about a product or service, a company policy, or a co-worker's idea. Remind students that their opinion will be taken more seriously when they can support it with reasons, facts, and logical arguments, not just generalizations. Have students brainstorm situations in the workplace in which they might be asked to give their opinion and support it.

Reading and Writing 4, page 200

Grammar: Adverb phrases of reason (10 minutes)

1. Read the information and examples about adverb clauses and phrases of reason.
2. Check comprehension: *What do adverb clauses of reason do? What is an example of a subordinator? How do you reduce an adverb clause with a simple verb? How do you reduce an adverb clause with a perfect verb?*

Skill Note

Adverb clauses of reason often occur before the main clause, as in the example *Because they heard the kipunji was rare, poachers began to visit the habitat.* Both clauses in this sentence have the same subject: poachers. When the subjects of both clauses are the same, there is no need to repeat the subject. Students can vary their sentences by changing adverb clauses to adverb phrases. For example: *Hearing that the kipunji was rare, poachers began to visit its habitat.*

Tip for Success (1 minute)

1. Read the tip aloud.
2. Explain: *One way to have more variety in your writing is to use both adverb phrases and adverb clauses. This will help you avoid using the same grammar structures over and over again.*

A (10 minutes)

1. Direct students to reduce each adverb clause to an adverb phrase.
2. Ask volunteers to write their sentences on the board and correct them together as a class.

Grammar A Answers, pp. 200–201

2. Having done so much research,….
3. Understanding the danger of disease,….
4. Realizing that people doubted the existence of the tribe,….
5. Having accepted that more contact with the tribespeople is inevitable,….

Reading and Writing 4, page 201

B (10 minutes)

1. Direct students to write the full adverb clause for each adverb phrase.
2. Elicit the answers from volunteers.

Grammar B Answers, p. 201

2. Because they recognized the importance of the discovery,
3. Because he (had) heard about the discovery of a new tribe,
4. Because they hope that they can save the kipunji,
5. Because they (had) found that the kipunji's DNA was unique,

For additional practice with adverb phrases of reason, have students visit *Q Online Practice.*

Unit Assignment: Write an opinion essay

Unit Question (5 minutes)

Refer students back to the ideas they discussed at the beginning of the unit about discoveries. Cue students by asking specific questions about the unit: *What are some good discoveries that have been made? What are some disadvantages of discoveries? How can you determine whether a discovery is good or not?*

Learning Outcome

1. Tie the Unit Assignment to the unit Learning Outcome. Say: *The outcome for this unit is to write an opinion essay. This Unit Assignment is going to let you show your skill in writing an opinion essay with supporting reasons as well as using adverb phrases of reason.*
2. Explain that you are going to use a rubric similar to their Self-Assessment checklist on p. 204 to grade their Unit Assignment. You can also share a copy of the Unit Assignment Rubric (on p. 87 of this *Teacher's Handbook*) with the students.

Reading and Writing 4, page 202

Plan and Write

Brainstorm

A (15 minutes)

1. Have students first note their ideas individually. Then direct them to work with a partner to complete the chart.
2. As pairs finish, have them choose one discovery and decide if it is a good or bad thing.

Tip for Success (1 minute)

1. Read the tip aloud.
2. Explain: *In an opinion essay, it is important to support your ideas with facts and examples. If you want your readers to agree with you, you need to give compelling reasons.*

Plan

B (20 minutes)

1. Tell students that they will write an outline to organize their essay. Read the steps together.
2. Direct students to work individually to complete their outline. Provide assistance as needed.

Reading and Writing 4, page 204

Write

C (20 minutes)

Direct students to use their outline to write their essay. Remind them to refer to the Self-Assessment checklist on p. 204.

Alternative Unit Assignments

Assign or have students choose one of these assignments to do instead of, or in addition to, the Unit Assignment.

1. Is the exploration of space worth the cost? Write an essay giving your opinion and support it with reasons.
2. If you could work in exploration or research, what field would you like to specialize in and why? Write an essay explaining your choice.

For an additional Unit Assignment, have students visit *Q Online Practice.*

Revise and Edit

Peer Review

A (15 minutes)

1. Pair students and direct them to read each other's work
2. Ask students to answer and discuss the questions.
3. Give students suggestions of helpful feedback: *Your first sentence really caught my attention. Remember to include an adverb phrase. You supported your ideas well in the third paragraph.*

Rewrite

B (10 minutes)

Students should review their partners' answers from A and rewrite their essays if necessary.

Edit

C (10 minutes)

1. Direct students to read and complete the Self-Assessment checklist. They should be prepared to hand in their work or discuss it in class.
2. Ask for a show of hands for how many students gave all or mostly *yes* answers.
3. Use the Unit Assignment Rubric on p. 87 in this *Teacher's Handbook* to score each student's assignment.
4. Alternatively, divide the class into large groups and have students read their essays to their group. Pass out copies of the Unit Assignment Rubric and have students grade each other.

▶ *Reading and Writing 4, page 205*

Track Your Success (5 minutes)

1. Have students circle the words they have learned in this unit. Suggest that students go back through the unit to review any words they have forgotten.
2. Have students check the skills they have mastered. If students need more practice to feel confident about their proficiency in a skill, point out the page numbers and encourage them to review.
3. Read the Learning Outcome aloud. Ask students if they feel that they have met the outcome.

Unit Assignment Rubric

Student name: ____

Date: ____________

Unit Assignment: *Write an opinion essay.*

20 points = Essay element was completely successful (at least 90% of the time).
15 points = Essay element was mostly successful (at least 70% of the time).
10 points = Essay element was partially successful (at least 50% of the time).
0 points = Essay element was not successful.

Write an Opinion Essay	20 points	15 points	10 points	0 points
Essay clearly expresses the student's opinion about the topic.				
Essay includes an introduction, multiple reasons, and a conclusion.				
Each reason is supported by facts, examples, or logical arguments.				
Adverb phrases of reason are used correctly (if included).				
Punctuation, grammar, and spelling are correct.				

Total points: ____________

Comments:

UNIT 9

Unit QUESTION

Have humans lost their connection to nature?

Humans and Nature

READING • taking episodic notes
VOCABULARY • metaphors
WRITING • varying sentence patterns
GRAMMAR • parallel structure and ellipsis

LEARNING OUTCOME

Relate a story about how people connect with nature in a positive or negative way.

Reading and Writing 4, pages 206–207

Preview the Unit

Learning Outcome

1. Ask for a volunteer to read the unit skills and the unit Learning Outcome.
2. Explain: *This is what you are expected to be able to do by the unit's end. The Learning Outcome explains how you are going to be evaluated. With this outcome in mind, you should focus on learning those skills (Reading, Vocabulary, Writing, Grammar) that will support your goal of relating a story about how people connect with nature. You can also act as a mentor in the classroom to help your classmates learn the skills and meet this Learning Outcome.*

A (15 minutes)

1. Ask students about their personal experiences: *How do you like to enjoy nature? What do you like to do?*
2. Put students in pairs or small groups to discuss the first two questions. Then call on volunteers to share their ideas. Ask: *Why is it easier to live in the city/country? Do you have any survival skills?*
3. Focus students' attention on the photo. Have a volunteer describe the photo to the class. Read the third question aloud. Elicit students' answers.

Preview the Unit A Answers, p. 207

Answers will vary. Sample answers:

1. It's easier to live in the city because you have everything you need.
2. If I were lost in the wilderness, I would not be able to survive. I don't know how to hunt for food.
3. The design of the house suggests a close relationship with nature because it is in the middle of the desert. / The design suggests a distant relationship with nature because it's very modern.

B (10 minutes)

1. Introduce the Unit Question: "Have humans lost their connection to nature?" Ask related information questions or questions about personal experience to help students prepare for answering the more abstract Unit Question. Ask: *How do people interact with nature today compared to in the past? Do you think that people now are more connected or less connected to nature than they were in the past? Why? How will humans' connection with nature be different in 50 years?*
2. Read the Unit Question aloud. Give students a minute to silently consider their answers. Then ask students who would answer *yes* to stand on one side of the room and students who would answer *no* to stand on the other side of the room.
3. Direct students to tell the person next to them their reasons for choosing the answer they did.
4. Call on volunteers from each side to share their opinions with the class.
5. After students have shared their opinions, provide an opportunity for anyone who would like to change sides to do so.
6. Ask to copy the Unit Question and make a note of their answers and their reasons. They will refer back to these notes at the end of the unit.

Preview the Unit B Answers, p. 207

Answers will vary. Sample answers:

Lower-level answer: Yes, we have lost our connection to nature because we get our food from supermarkets.

On-level answer: I think humans have lost their connection to nature because many people live in cities, where it's difficult to find nature.

Higher-level answer: In my opinion, humans have lost their connection to nature. We have many modern conveniences, such as supermarkets, so people no longer need to grow their own food.

The Q Classroom (5 minutes)

CD2, Track 11

1. Play *The Q Classroom*. Use the example from the audio to help students continue the conversation. Ask: *How did the students answer the question? Do you agree or disagree with their ideas? Why?*
2. Discuss Yuna's point about how nature doesn't let us forget about it. Ask students to give recent examples of natural disasters, either locally or from the news.

Reading and Writing 4, page 208

C (15 minutes)

1. Tell students to read and complete the survey.
2. Have students compare answers with a partner.

MULTILEVEL OPTION

Higher-level students will likely finish Activity C before their lower-level classmates. Pair higher-level students so they can compare answers as they finish. Then instruct them to write sentences comparing their answers to their partner's. For example, *I often check the weather forecast, but Rania never does* or *Sam and I both love camping.*

Preview the Unit C Answers, p. 208

Answers will vary.

D (5 minutes)

1. Students should calculate their scores and read the results. Direct partners to discuss whether or not they agree with the results.
2. Elicit responses from volunteers.

Preview the Unit D Answers, p. 208

Answers will vary.

EXPANSION ACTIVITY: Group Survey (15 minutes)

1. Expand on Activities C and D on p. 208 by having students write a short paragraph in response to their survey results.
2. Students should state whether or not they agree with the results and give reasons.
3. Have students share their paragraphs with a partner. Call on volunteers to read their paragraphs aloud.

READING

Reading and Writing 4, pages 209

READING 1: Survival School

VOCABULARY (15 minutes)

1. Ask volunteers to read the bold words and their definitions. Provide examples of the words in context. Model the pronunciation of each word and have students repeat.
2. Direct students to complete each sentence with the correct vocabulary word.
3. Have volunteers read the completed sentences.

MULTILEVEL OPTION

Pair lower-level students and provide them with additional sample sentences using the vocabulary words. For example, *I like teachers who are **accessible** outside of class to answer questions. Hunting animals does not **appeal** to me; it seems very cruel. She felt **apprehensive** about starting her new job because she didn't know anybody.*

Instruct higher-level students to write sentences with the vocabulary words. Ask for volunteers to write their sentences on the board. Go over the sentences as a class, focusing on the use of the vocabulary words.

Vocabulary Answers, pp. 209–210

1. appeal; **2.** indicate; **3.** shelter;
4. ravenous; **5.** reliant; **6.** intrigued;
7. brutality; **8.** stranded; **9.** accessible;
10. devour; **11.** laborious; **12.** apprehensive

For additional practice with the vocabulary, have students visit *Q Online Practice*.

Reading and Writing 4, page 210

PREVIEW READING 1 (5 minutes)

1. Read the introduction aloud. Direct students to discuss their answer with a partner.
2. Tell students they should review their answer after reading.

Preview Reading 1 Answer, p. 210

Answers will vary. Sample answers:
Someone might want to take a survival course in order to be prepared for a natural disaster. / Some people are interested in hunting or learning new skills like orienteering (following a compass).

Reading 1 Background Note

The Wildwood Survival website discusses wilderness survival in terms of living in harmony with nature. The website lists several survival schools, many of which have a slightly different focus. For example, the Wilderness Awareness School in Washington focuses on teaching children an awareness and appreciation for nature. Adventure Out in California pledges to help you achieve your wildest adventures in the outdoors. Survival in the Bush, Inc. in Ontario, Canada, teaches you not to fight against nature, but to cooperate with her.

READ (20 minutes)

CD2 Track 12

1. Instruct students to read the article. Remind them to refer to the glossed words as they read.
2. When students have finished reading, answer any questions they may have about the article or additional vocabulary. Then play the audio and have students follow along.

Reading and Writing 4, page 212

MAIN IDEAS (15 minutes)

1. Have students complete the activity individually.
2. Direct students to compare their answers with a partner, going back to the article to check their answers.
3. Elicit the answers from volunteers. Ask: *What do you think of the survival experience? Is it something that you would like to try?*

Main Ideas Answers, pp. 212–213

1. how to survive if a day hike goes wrong
2. men and women who want to be less reliant
3. make a shelter
4. look for water and food
5. lit a fire and used pine needles for insulation
6. hungry and tired, but proud

Reading and Writing 4, page 213

DETAILS

A (10 minutes)

1. Direct students to check the correct person for each statement.
2. Then have students compare answers with a partner. Remind them to refer back to the article to check their answers.
3. Go over the answers as a class.

Details A Answers, p. 213

1. Elliot Spaulding; **2.** Lee Posner; **3.** Tony Nester; **4.** Tony Nester; **5.** Lee Posner; **6.** Elliot Spaulding

B (5 minutes)

1. Direct students to mark each statement *T* or *F*. Remind students to correct the false statements to make them true.
2. Have students compare answers with a partner before discussing the answers as a class.

Details B Answers, p. 213

1. T;
2. F (Students have had serious accidents and have even died.);
3. T;
4. F (For food, they found wild onions, cranberries, and acorns.);
5. T

For additional practice with reading comprehension, have students visit *Q Online Practice*.

Reading and Writing 4, page 214

WHAT DO YOU THINK? (20 minutes)

1. Ask students to read the questions and reflect on their answers.
2. Seat students in small groups and assign roles: a group leader to make sure everyone contributes, a note-taker to record the group's ideas, a reporter to share the group's ideas with the class, and a timekeeper to watch the clock.
3. Give students five minutes to discuss the questions. Call time if conversations are winding down. Allow them an extra minute or two if necessary.
4. Call on each group's reporter to share ideas with the class.
5. Have each student choose one of the questions and write for 5-10 minutes in response.
6. Call on volunteers to share their responses.

What Do You Think? Activity Answers, p. 214

Answers will vary. Sample answers:

1. I would like to take a survival course because I think it would be interesting to learn how to catch food and cook it. / I'm not sure if a survival course has any real benefits because in today's world, you can just go to the store to get food.
2. I like to feel independent. I would like to have land so I could raise animals and grow my own food. That way I wouldn't have to depend on others to eat.

MULTILEVEL OPTION:

As students share their answers to the questions, note on the board any related vocabulary or ideas that come up. This way, lower-level students will have a list of key words and ideas to use as they write their response to one of the questions.

Reading Skill: Taking episodic notes (5 minutes)

1. Ask for volunteers to read the information about taking episodic notes.
2. Check comprehension by asking questions: *When would you take episodic notes? What three things should you do when taking episodic notes?*

Tip for Success (3 minutes)

1. Ask a volunteer to read the tip aloud.
2. Ask: *When do you take notes? What kind of information do you write? What do you do with that information when you're finished?*
3. Encourage students to revisit their notes when they study or prepare for a test. Tell them that reorganizing their notes will help them to remember the most important information.

A (5 minutes)

1. Direct students to read the episodic notes and write the correct paragraph number.
2. Elicit the answers from volunteers.

Reading Skill A Answers, p. 214

1. Paragraph 1
2. Paragraph 12

Reading and Writing 4, page 215

B (15 minutes)

1. Direct students to take episodic notes for paragraphs 7–11. Remind them to use the information and examples on p. 214 as a guide.
2. After students compare notes with a partner, call on volunteers to share their notes with the class. Highlight similarities or differences in the notes.

Reading Skill B Answers, p. 215

Answers will vary.

For additional practice with taking episodic notes, have students visit *Q Online Practice*.

Learning Outcome

Use the Learning Outcome to frame the purpose and relevance of Reading 1. Ask: *What did you learn from Reading 1 that prepares you to relate a story about how people connect with nature in a positive or negative way?* (Students learned about a survival school that teaches people how to survive in the wilderness. They may want to use some of these ideas when they write their narrative essays.)

READING 2: Man Against Nature

VOCABULARY (15 minutes)

1. Tell students to read each sentence and try to guess the meaning of the bold word from context. Then they should write each bold word next to the correct definition.
2. Call on students to read the vocabulary words and definitions aloud.

Vocabulary Answers, p. 216

a. handle; **b.** maintenance;
c. seek; **d.** resort to;
e. siege; **f.** battle;
g. territory; **h.** pest;
i. turn out to be; **j.** nuisance;
k. hysterical; **l.** invade

For additional practice with the vocabulary, have students visit *Q Online Practice*.

Reading and Writing 4, page 216

PREVIEW READING 2 (10 minutes)

1. Read the introduction aloud.
2. Direct students to write their ideas. Have them share their answers in small groups.
3. Tell students they should review their answers after reading.

Preview Reading 2 Answers, p. 216

Answers will vary. Sample answers:
One problem that people may have with native wildlife is that the animals may get into their trash containers. / If people have house pets, the native animals might harm, or even kill, their pets.

Reading 2 Background Note

Many cities are developing plans to help their residents live in harmony with urban wildlife and educate them about the differences between wild animals and urban wildlife.

Some dos and don'ts to follow if you encounter urban wildlife include: don't separate a mother from her babies, don't ever feed animals, do keep your garbage well contained, and do call for professional help if you have a conflict with urban wildlife.

Reading and Writing 4, page 217

READ (20 minutes)

CD2 Track 13

1. Instruct students to read the article. Remind them to refer to the glossed words as they read.
2. When students have finished reading, answer any questions they may have about the article or additional vocabulary.
3. Play the audio and have students follow along.
4. Explain how *boy* is used in an exclamatory sense in the last sentence in paragraph 2.

Reading and Writing 4, page 218

MAIN IDEAS (10 minutes)

1. Direct students to circle the best answer for each question.
2. Elicit the answers from volunteers.

Main Ideas Answers, pp. 218–219

1. c; **2.** b; **3.** a; **4.** c; **5.** c

Reading and Writing 4, page 219

DETAILS (10 minutes)

1. Direct students to mark each statement *T* or *F*.
2. Have students compare answers with a partner. Remind them to refer back to the article to check their answers.
3. Go over the answers with the class. Elicit corrections for the false statements.

Details Answers, p. 219

1. T; **2.** F; **3.** T; **4.** F; **5.** F; **6.** T; **7.** T

web For additional practice with reading comprehension, have students visit *Q Online Practice*.

Q WHAT DO YOU THINK?

A (15 minutes)

1. Ask students to read the questions and reflect on their answers.
2. Seat students in small groups and assign roles: a group leader to make sure everyone contributes, a note-taker to record the group's ideas, a reporter to share the group's ideas with the class, and a timekeeper to watch the clock.
3. Give students five minutes to discuss the questions. Call time if conversations are winding down. Allow them an extra minute or two if necessary.
4. Have students choose one of the questions and write a paragraph in response.
5. Call on volunteers to share their responses.

What Do You Think? Activity A Answers, p. 219

Answers will vary. Sample answers:

1. I think using the word "war" is an exaggeration. I think the writer decided to use this word to add drama to the article.

2. I believe that we must respect animals and preserve their natural habitats. If we build on their land, we should be sure to plan for green spaces where they can live. If we don't, they will interfere with our lives as much as we interfere with theirs.

Reading and Writing 4, page 220

B (10 minutes)

1. Tell the students that they should think about both Reading 1 and Reading 2 as they discuss the questions with their group.
2. Call on each group to share their ideas.

What Do You Think? Activity B Answers, p. 220

Answers will vary. Sample answers:

1. I feel comfortable around many different animals. Some animals, like bears, scare me, though. I think this is because I have not been around big, wild animals like that.

2. I think mankind's relationship with nature is unhealthy. We only take from nature, and we don't do enough to give back.

Critical Thinking Tip (1 minute)

1. Ask a volunteer to read the tip aloud.
2. Explain: *When you are asked to give reasons for your decision, or opinion, think about what you know about the topic from texts you have read or from your own experiences. If your reasons are based on something you know, they will be more convincing.*

Learning Outcome

Use the Learning Outcome to frame the purpose and relevance of Readings 1 and 2. Ask: *What did you learn from Readings 1 and 2 that prepares you to relate a story about how people connect with nature in a positive or negative way?* (Students learned how people interact with nature and encounter wildlife in both remote natural areas and urban settings. They may want to use some of these ideas when they write their narrative essays.)

Vocabulary Skill: Metaphors (10 minutes)

1. Ask volunteers to read the information about metaphors.
2. Check comprehension: *What is an example of a metaphor from the reading? How is a metaphor different from a literal statement? Why are metaphors used?*

Skill Note

Many common idiomatic expressions are metaphors in English. Introducing students to idioms, which they may have heard before, may help them to understand the concept of metaphor.

There are many metaphors to describe people. When someone has a lot of money, we can say that he is "rolling in dough." When someone is very special to us, we might say that person is "the apple of my eye." Similarly, if someone is very brave, we can say, "She has the heart of a lion."

The weather is another source for many idiomatic metaphors. If we are having trouble remembering something, we might say, "My memory is foggy," meaning that it is unclear. Additionally, when something is easy for us, we may say, "It is a breeze."

A (10 minutes)

1. Direct students to underline the words or phrases that show a comparison with war.
2. Go over the answers with the class. You may want to project the page to show the underlining.

Vocabulary Skill A Answers, p. 220

1. Any four from the following whole phrases (underlined) or the words alone (bold):

This is not a new situation. Consider this: humans took the **territory** through urbanization, but nature has sent in its **troops** in the form of skunks, squirrels, and bears to win it back by **siege.** Deer have **occupied** private lawns, golf courses and playing fields. Bears have begun to search through trash cans in the western part of the state, while coyotes and geese have **taken hold of** the central and southern regions. And squirrels **are invading** the newcomers—otherwise known as humans—everywhere.

Reading and Writing 4, page 221

B (15 minutes)

1. Direct students to read the instructions and to write their sentences with a partner.
2. Then call on volunteers to share their sentences.

Vocabulary Skill B Answers, p. 221

All situations in the box could be described using the vocabulary of war.

Answers will vary. Sample answers:

1. Gardening: Weeds have **occupied** my garden.
2. Shopping in a crowded store: Shoppers are **invading** sales racks everywhere.
3. Parking the car: I've **taken hold of** a great spot right next to the entrance.
4. Tennis match: I lost my World Champion title in 2006 but I was able to **win it back by siege** in 2007.

Tip for Success (1 minute)

1. Read the tip aloud.
2. Explain: *A metaphor does not use a word's literal meaning. For example, in the metaphor "She has the heart of a lion," we are not saying that a woman has an actual lion's heart. We are comparing her bravery to the bravery of a lion. Idioms are often metaphors because they do not use language literally either.*

C (10 minutes)

1. Have students work with a partner to identify the metaphors. Encourage them to use their dictionaries for help.
2. Circulate around the room to help students figure out the meanings of the metaphors.
3. Call on volunteers to share their answers with the class. Write several of the metaphors on the board as you discuss their meanings.

Vocabulary Skill C Answers, p. 221

Whole phrases (underlined) or the words alone (bold):

1. He teaches a growing **band of people** intrigued with primitive technology.
2. His face was apprehensive as he **marched into** the trees.
3. We then **littered** the floor inside the shelter with pine needles.
4. The cold ground will **suck** the 98.6 degrees of temperature right out of your body.
5. The icy cold **stabbed into** our clothing.
6. **A blanket of darkness** descended just as the fire we eventually started **roared to life.**
7. We either **roasted** in the shelter, or froze when we fell asleep and the fire died.
8. Our trip was only **a taste**, but it demonstrated the brutality of life without easily accessible food

For additional practice with metaphors, have students visit *Q Online Practice*.

Critical Q: Expansion Activity

Use Metaphors

Activity C on p. 221 asks students to identify the metaphors and explain their meanings. Students must first recognize the metaphors as having non-literal word meanings and then explain the meaning of each metaphor based on context or by using a dictionary.

To apply their understanding of the metaphors in Activity C, have students work in pairs to write sentences that use the metaphors in a new context. Have volunteers share their sentences with the class.

Reading and Writing 4, page 222

WRITING

Writing Skill: Varying sentence patterns (10 minutes)

1. Read the information about varying sentence patterns. Have volunteers read the examples.
2. Check comprehension: *What is one way to add variety to your writing? What's the difference between active and passive sentences? When should you use quoted speech?*

Reading and Writing 4, page 223

A (20 minutes)

1. Direct students to rewrite the paragraphs using the different methods.
2. Have students share their changes with a partner before discussing them as a class.
3. You may want to type out the answers below and hand them out or project them so students can compare them with their own changes.

Writing Skill A Answers, p. 223

Answers will vary. Sample answers:

1. Last weekend was the longest weekend of my life. I attended a short survival course, and it is something that I will never forget. When I woke up very early on Saturday, it was still dark. I wanted to go back to sleep. I left my house reluctantly, and I drove to the school at the edge of the desert. By the time I arrived at 8 a.m., the desert was already hot. I felt nervous, but I didn't want to show it. After the other students arrived, the instructor came out to greet us.
2. The instructor asked us to listen to him carefully. He said, "This course is tough but worthwhile." He explained that first we would learn survival techniques in the classroom, like finding food, building a shelter, and building a fire. Then after lunch, he said we would go out to the desert. He said he hoped we were all ready for this. The person next to me whispered, "I'm not sure that I am."
3. The class was held in a clean, modern classroom. I had lots of fun. We were shown a number of different ways of surviving in the desert, and we were all fascinated by the techniques. I asked many questions, and the class had some good discussions. Finally we were given a test using a computer program. It had been designed to check if someone could hike in the desert safely. We all passed the test. Then we were led out of the building and into the desert. We were allowed to take only a bottle of water and a compass.

Tip for Success (1 minute)

1. Ask a volunteer to read the tip aloud.
2. Explain: *This writing skill is supposed to help you create more variety in your writing, not overwhelm you with work. You do not need to vary every sentence in each paragraph. Just be sure to use a variety of patterns overall.*

B (15 minutes)

1. Direct students to rewrite the paragraphs. Then direct them to compare their paragraphs with a partner and discuss their changes.
2. You may want to type out the answers below and hand them out or project them so students can compare them with their own changes.

Writing Skill B Answers, pp. 223–224

Answers will vary. Sample answers:

We hiked through the desert for miles. We were scorched by the sun and blinded by the wind. The instructor told us to do our best and push ourselves to the limit. Because we wanted to impress him, we were motivated to keep going.

We searched for food in the desert, and we found an edible plant (that is) called a barrel cactus. We also caught a lizard that can be boiled and eaten, but no one wanted to eat it.

Eventually, the instructor said that we were going to split into two teams. He asked us who wanted to be a team leader. I was exhausted, but for some reason I answered, "I do!" My team built a shelter, and the other team built a fire. The fire was placed near the shelter to keep us warm during the night.

We were all exhausted by the hard work, so we slept deeply. We were woken by the light of dawn the next morning. It was the first time that I had slept in the desert. I felt tired, sore, hungry, and very proud.

For additional practice with varying sentence patterns, have students visit *Q Online Practice*.

Reading and Writing 4, page 224

Grammar: Parallel structure and ellipsis (10 minutes)

1. Ask volunteers to read the information and examples aloud.
2. Check comprehension: *What is parallel structure? Can you think of another example using two adjectives? What is ellipsis? When can you use ellipsis?*

Skill Note

Language learners can improve their writing by varying their sentence patterns (as described in the Writing Skill on p. 223) and utilizing parallel structure and ellipsis.

Encourage students to recognize parallel structure and ellipsis by having them search for examples in texts they read in class. As they become more familiar with how these devices are used, they will feel more comfortable using them in their own writing.

Reading and Writing 4, page 225

A (10 minutes)

1. Direct students to read the sentences and correct the errors. Then have partners compare answers.
2. Elicit the revised sentences from volunteers. You may want to project the page to highlight the corrections.

Grammar A Answers, p. 225

1. Pedro is good at **reading** maps and following trails.
2. Jake likes to cycle and ~~to~~ climb mountains.
3. If someone needs help, you should be brave but not ~~**be**~~ foolish.
4. In a survival situation, it's essential to build a shelter, keep warm, and ~~finding~~ **find** water.
5. The instructor didn't take part in the search for food but ~~he~~ watched from a distance.
6. The students listened carefully, watched the instructor, and ~~**have**~~ learned how to make a fire.
7. Chang wasn't happy in the survival course; he was always complaining or ~~got~~ **getting** lost.
8. In most cities, you can visit museums or ~~you~~ go shopping in stores.

B (10 minutes)

1. Direct students to complete the sentences individually. Remind them to look at the information on p. 224 for help.
2. Have volunteers write their sentences on the board. Correct any errors as a class.

Grammar B Answers, p. 225

Answers will vary. Sample answers:

2. …advantages of spending a lot of time outdoors.
3. …build their own shelter.
4. …went camping in the mountains.
5. …in a desert.
6. …go for a walk.
7. …take a long bath.

For additional practice with parallel structure and ellipsis, have students visit *Q Online Practice*.

Reading and Writing 4, page 226

Unit Assignment: Write a narrative essay

Unit Question (5 minutes)

Refer students back to the ideas they discussed at the beginning of the unit about humans' connection with nature. Cue students if necessary by asking specific questions about the content of the unit: *Do you feel comfortable in nature? Could you survive in nature for several days if you needed to? What do you remember about the battle with the animals that we read about?*

21ST CENTURY SKILLS

Since a large percentage of communication in the workplace takes place through email, it's imperative that employees know how to clearly express their ideas in writing. Explain to students that their writing will be clearer and more interesting if they use varied sentence patterns. Say: *The first impression you might make on a company may be in a cover letter or email. This letter must explain your experiences and qualifications in a clear, interesting way and set you apart from other applicants.* Discuss other forms of written communication in the workplace in which it would be important for employees to vary their writing.

Learning Outcome

1. Tie the Unit Assignment to the unit Learning Outcome. Say: *The outcome for this unit is to write a narrative essay. This Unit Assignment is going to let you show your skill at writing an essay using a variety of sentences, parallel structure, and ellipsis.*
2. Explain that you are going to use a rubric similar to their Self-Assessment checklist on p. 228 to grade their Unit Assignment. You can also share a copy of the Unit Assignment Rubric (on p. 98 of this *Teacher's Handbook*) with the students.

Plan and Write

Brainstorm

A (15 minutes)

1. Have students work with a partner to fill in their T-chart.
2. If students have trouble coming up with ideas, elicit ideas from volunteers and list them on the board. This might help students think of something to write about.
3. Help students elaborate on their chosen ideas. Remind them of how to write episodic notes.

Tip for Success (1 minute)

1. Ask a volunteer to read the tip aloud.
2. Ask students why the tip is helpful. They should recognize that their supporting ideas must all be relevant and important to their main idea.

Plan

B (15 minutes)

1. Remind students about the usefulness of writing an outline.
2. Direct students to follow the directions to plan their essay. Encourage them to look at the Writing Skill box on p. 72.
3. Circulate around the room to help guide students through this process and answer questions.

Reading and Writing 4, page 227

Write

C (20 minutes)

1. Tell students to refer to the Self-Assessment checklist on page 228 before they begin writing.
2. Then direct students to write their essays, following their outline from Activity B.

Alternative Unit Assignments

Assign or have students choose one of these assignments to do instead of, or in addition to, the Unit Assignment.

1. An architect is proposing for a new city to be built that will be sealed off from the natural world by a large transparent dome. Inside the dome, there will be no animals, birds, insects or plants. Write an essay explaining the advantages and disadvantages of the proposal in your opinion.
2. Write a blog entry about the role of nature in your life. Explain whether or not you are satisfied with the amount of time you find for nature. If you are not satisfied, say what changes you would like to make.

web For an additional Unit Assignment, have students visit *Q Online Practice*.

Reading and Writing 4, page 228

Revise and Edit

Peer Review

A (15 minutes)

1. Pair students and direct them to read each other's work.
2. Ask students to answer and discuss the questions.
3. Give students suggestions of helpful feedback: *I like the episode you described in the second paragraph. Don't forget to vary your sentence patterns in the first paragraph. There was a problem with the verb tense in the last sentence.*

Rewrite

B (10 minutes)

Students should review their partners' answers from A and rewrite their paragraphs if necessary.

Edit

C (10 minutes)

1. Direct students to read and complete the Self-Assessment checklist. They should be prepared to hand in their work or discuss it in class.
2. Ask for a show of hands for how many students gave all or mostly *yes* answers.
3. Use the Unit Assignment Rubric on p. 98 in this *Teacher's Handbook* to score each student's essay.
4. Alternatively, divide the class into large groups and have students read their essays to their group. Pass out copies of the Unit Assignment Rubric and have students grade each other.

Reading and Writing 4, page 228

Track Your Success (5 minutes)

1. Have students circle the words they have learned in this unit. Suggest that students go back through the unit to review any words they have forgotten.
2. Have students check the skills they have mastered. If students need more practice to feel confident about their proficiency in a skill, point out the page numbers and encourage them to review.
3. Read the Learning Outcome aloud. Ask students if they feel that they have met the outcome.

Unit Assignment Rubric

Student name: ________________________________

Date: __________

Unit Assignment: *Write a narrative essay.*

20 points = Essay element was completely successful (at least 90% of the time).
15 points = Essay element was mostly successful (at least 70% of the time).
10 points = Essay element was partially successful (at least 50% of the time).
0 points = Essay element was not successful.

Write a Narrative Essay	20 points	15 points	10 points	0 points
Essay tells a story about humans and their connection to nature.				
Essay includes events that are told in the order they happened.				
Essay includes varied sentence patterns.				
Parallel structure and ellipsis are used correctly.				
Punctuation, spelling, and grammar are correct.				

Total points: __________

Comments:

UNIT **10** *Unit* QUESTION
Why is it important to play?

Child's Play

READING • identifying counterarguments and refutations
VOCABULARY • collocations with prepositions
WRITING • writing a persuasive essay
GRAMMAR • adverb clauses of concession

LEARNING OUTCOME

Make arguments to persuade readers that video games are helpful or harmful to children.

Reading and Writing 4, pages 230–231

Preview the Unit

Learning Outcome

1. Ask for a volunteer to read the unit skills and the unit Learning Outcome.
2. Explain: *This is what you are expected to be able to do by the unit's end. The Learning Outcome explains how you are going to be evaluated. With this outcome in mind, you should focus on learning those skills (Reading, Vocabulary, Writing, and Grammar) that will support your goal of making arguments to persuade readers that video games are helpful or harmful to children. You can also act as a mentor in the classroom to help your classmates learn the skills and meet this Learning Outcome.*

A (15 minutes)

1. Ask students: *Do you have young children, siblings, or cousins? How much time do they spend playing? How much time do adults spend playing?*
2. Put students in pairs or small groups to discuss the first two questions. Then call on volunteers to share their ideas with the class. Ask: *What are some of the games that both you and your partner played as children? What are some things adults do to play?*
3. Focus students' attention on the photo. Have a volunteer describe the photo to the class. Read the third question aloud. Elicit students' answers.

Preview the Unit A Answers, p. 231
Answers will vary. Sample answers:
1. When I was a child, I liked to play hide and seek. It was exciting to run around and look for my friends.
2. Yes, adults need to "play." Playing for adults may mean doing a hobby or going to a movie.
3. Yes, this looks enjoyable to me because I love rides. My favorite rides are roller coasters.

B (5 minutes)

1. Introduce the Unit Question: "Why is it important to play?" Ask related information questions or questions about personal experience to help students prepare for answering the more abstract Unit Question. For example, ask: *What do you like to do for fun on the weekends? Is your idea of fun changing as you get older?*
2. Put students in small groups and give each group a piece of poster paper and a marker.
3. Read the Unit Question aloud. Give students a minute to silently consider their answers to the question. Tell students to pass the paper and the marker around the group. Direct each group member to write a different answer to the question. Encourage them to help one another.
4. Ask each group to choose a reporter to read the answers to the class. Point out similarities and differences among the answers. If answers from different groups are similar, make a group list that incorporates the answers. Post the list for students to refer to later in the unit.

Preview the Unit B Answers, p. 231
Answers will vary. Sample answers:
Lower-level answer: It is important to play because we need to have fun.
On-level answer: It is important to play because our bodies and minds need a break from our daily lives.
Higher-level answer: Play is important because our bodies and our minds need a break from the stress and routines in our daily lives. It also gives us something to look forward to.

The Q Classroom (5 minutes)

CD2 Track 14

1. Play *The Q Classroom*. Use the example from the audio to help students continue the conversation. Ask: *How did the students answer the question? Do you agree or disagree with their ideas? Why?*
2. Ask students to write 2-3 sentences explaining their opinion. Tell them they should look back at their opinion at the end of the unit.

Reading and Writing 4, page 232

C (10 minutes)

1. Tell students to read the quotations and think about their answers to the questions. Then have students discuss the questions with a partner.
2. Elicit answers from volunteers.

MULTILEVEL OPTION

Have higher-level students write a short paragraph in response to one of the quotations. Have them choose the quotation that is most interesting to them and explain whether they agree or disagree with it.

Preview the Unit C Answers, p. 232

Answers will vary. Sample answers:

1. If you do a job that you like, it doesn't feel like work.
2. Playing will keep you young.
3. People find peace of mind through their work.
4. You can learn more about people by watching them having fun for a short time than when you're having a serious talk with them for a long time.
5. Every person has an inner-child who wants to have fun and play.
6. To children, play is important business.

D (5 minutes)

Have partners discuss their favorite quotation. Then elicit favorite quotations from volunteers.

Preview the Unit D Answers, p. 208

Answers will vary.

EXPANSION ACTIVITY: Personal Profile (20 minutes)

1. Tell students to choose one quotation from Activity C that reminds them of someone they know. They should choose a person whose life either supports or contradicts the quotation.
2. Have partners talk about the people they chose and ask questions to get more details.
3. Then have students write for 10 minutes about the person and the quotation.
4. Call on volunteers to share what they wrote.

READING

Reading and Writing 4, page 233

READING 1: The Promise of Play

VOCABULARY (15 minutes)

1. Have students read each sentence and try to guess the meaning of the word in bold.
2. Then students should write the word next to the correct definition.
3. Elicit the answers from volunteers.

MULTILEVEL OPTION

Assist lower-level students with the task. Provide additional sample sentences using the vocabulary words. For example, *I like to **incorporate** 20 minutes of quiet time into my morning routine. The football player needed **therapy** because he had hurt his knee. I feel **conflicted** about what to study in college; I really love math, but I think engineering will help me to find a better job.*

Have higher-level students write an additional sentence for each vocabulary word. Have volunteers write their sentences on the board. Correct the sentences with the class, focusing on the use of the words rather than other grammatical issues.

Vocabulary Answers, pp. 233–234

a. catalyst;	**b.** beneficial;	**c.** grim;
d. give in to;	**e.** incorporate;	**f.** strive;
g. mundane;	**h.** therapy;	**i.** conflicted;
j. skeptic;	**k.** innovative;	**l.** rigid

For additional practice with the vocabulary, have students visit *Q Online Practice*.

Reading and Writing 4, page 234

PREVIEW READING 1 (10 minutes)

1. Read the introduction and ask students to think about their answers to the question.
2. Have students discuss their ideas in small groups.
3. Call on each group to share ideas with the class.
4. Tell students they should review their answers after reading.

Preview Reading 1 Answer, p. 234
Answers will vary.

Reading 1 Background Note

Dr. Stuart Brown argues that play is essential for both children and adults. In this sense, the term *play* may include activities such as reading, playing a musical instrument, or inventing games with a friend. In his blog, Dr. Brown notes that playing provides us with a sense of control over our lives.

Like Dr. Brown, Dr. Peter Gray, a research professor of psychology at Boston College, makes the connection between play time and our sense of control over our lives. In an article for *Psychology Today,* Dr. Gray discussed how the decline in children's play time may be linked to an increase in anxiety and depression among children. Dr. Gray believes that over-scheduling children in organized activities and not giving them enough free play time may be one of the reasons that we are seeing an eight-fold increase in depression and anxiety among high school students.

READ (20 minutes)

CD2, Track 15

1. Instruct students to read the article. Remind them to refer to the glossed words as they read.
2. When students have finished reading, answer any questions they may have about the article or additional vocabulary.
3. Play the audio and have students follow along.

Reading and Writing 4, page 236

MAIN IDEAS (5 minutes)

1. Direct students to check the statements that the author would agree with.
2. Call on volunteers to share their answers with the class. Ask them to support their answers with information from the article.

Main Ideas Answers, p. 236
Checked: 1, 2, 4, and 7.

DETAILS (10 minutes)

1. Direct students to answer the questions.
2. Then have them compare answers with a partner. Remind students to refer back to the article to check their answers.
3. Go over the answers with the class.

Details Answers, p. 236

1. Fortune 500 companies, people who are clinically depressed, and groups of parents
2. Any three of the following: It can make us happier. It can make us more productive. It can help us to maintain social relationships. It helps us become creative, innovative people.
3. Any three of the following: movies, art, music, jokes, dramatic stories, flirting, daydreaming, comedy, irony
4. Any two of the following: how the world works, how friends interact, the mystery and excitement of the world
5. Any two of the following: They feel guilty. They think it is unproductive or a waste of time. It doesn't teach a skill, make money, or get on the boss's good side.

web For additional practice with reading comprehension, have students visit *Q Online Practice*.

WHAT DO YOU THINK? (20 minutes)

1. Ask students to read the questions and reflect on their answers.
2. Seat students in small groups and assign roles: a group leader to make sure everyone contributes, a note-taker to record the group's ideas, a reporter to share the group's ideas with the class, and a timekeeper to watch the clock. Give students five minutes to discuss the questions.
3. Call on each group's reporter to share ideas with the class.
4. Have each student choose one of the questions and write for 5-10 minutes in response.
5. Call on volunteers to share their responses.

MULTILEVEL OPTION:

Put students in mixed-ability pairs for the discussion. Higher-level students' answers can serve as a model for lower-level students. Then have the pairs choose the same question and write their response together, with the higher-level student doing the writing. Remind them that they both should include ideas in the response.

What Do You Think? Activity Answers, p. 236
Answers will vary. Sample answers:

1. Play is definitely a catalyst for me. When I do what I love, which is play volleyball, I always feel energized.
2. I agree with the author because if we didn't have fun things to look forward to, every day would be the same.

Learning Outcome

Use the Learning Outcome to frame the purpose and relevance of Reading 1. Ask: *What did you learn from Reading 1 that prepares you to persuade your readers that video games are helpful or harmful to children?* (Students learned about the importance of play and how it is beneficial in our lives. They may want to use some of these ideas when they do their Unit Assignments.)

Reading and Writing 4, page 237

Reading Skill: Identifying counterarguments and refutations

(15 minutes)

1. Ask for volunteers to read the information about counterarguments and refutations.
2. Highlight the clauses or expressions that show a counterargument vs. a refutation. Provide any additional examples.
3. Check comprehension: *What is a counterargument? How can you recognize a counterargument? What is a refutation?*
4. Direct students to work individually to match the counterarguments and refutations.
5. Have students compare their answers with a partner before discussing them as a class.

Reading Skill Answers, p. 237

1. f; Some people say that; but the fact is that
2. c; Some people argue that; The truth is, however, that
3. e; There are those who question; On the contrary, studies have shown that
4. a; Some think that; That is not the case
5. d; Many claim that; In reality
6. b; Some experts believe that; but, in fact

Tip for Success (1 minute)

1. Ask a volunteer to read the tip aloud.
2. Explain: *When you read a text, look for arguments, counterarguments, and refutations to figure out how the author feels about the topic.*

For additional practice with identifying counterarguments and refutations, have students visit *Q Online Practice*.

Reading and Writing 4, page 238

READING 2: Child's Play

VOCABULARY (15 minutes)

1. Direct students to read the vocabulary words and the definitions. Answer any questions about meaning and provide examples of the words in context. Model the pronunciation of each word and have students repeat.
2. Direct students to complete each sentence with a vocabulary word.
3. Call on volunteers to read the sentences aloud.

Vocabulary Answers, pp. 238–239

1. predetermined; **2.** inhibit;
3. evident; **4.** regulate;
5. impulsively; **6.** subtle;
7. consequently; **8.** conduct;
9. structured; **10.** vital;
11. complex

For additional practice with the vocabulary, have students visit *Q Online Practice*.

Reading and Writing 4, page 239

PREVIEW READING 2 (5 minutes)

1. Read the introduction and have students check the sentences.
2. Call on students to share their ideas.
3. Tell students they should review their answers after reading.

Preview Reading 2 Answers, p. 239

Answers will vary.

Reading 2 Background Note

Pretend play gives children a chance to self-regulate. Self-regulation happens when children are responsible for controlling their own behavior and can resist acting impulsively. Self-regulation may be something as simple as sitting quietly and focusing on one activity (like reading a book) for an extended period of time. Many adults, including teachers, complain that children have short attention spans and are not able to sit still for very long. The ability to self-regulate is important for children who are in a classroom environment for the first time. Children's past experiences regulating their own behavior may help them adjust to new expectations, such as sitting quietly for long periods of time, in the classroom.

Reading and Writing 4, page 240

READ (20 minutes)

CD2, Track 16

1. Instruct students to read the article. Remind them to refer to the glossed words as they read.
2. When students have finished reading, answer any questions they may have about the article or additional vocabulary.
3. Play the audio and have students follow along.

Reading and Writing 4, page 241

MAIN IDEAS

A (5 minutes)

1. Ask students to check the main idea.
2. Elicit the main idea from the class.

Main Ideas A Answer, p. 241

2. Young children need opportunities to pretend play because it helps them build language and social skills and learn to self-regulate

Reading and Writing 4, page 242

B (15 minutes)

1. Direct students to complete the chart.
2. Have students compare answers with a partner. If they disagree on something, they should go back to the article to check their answers.
3. You may want to write the main ideas on the board as you elicit them from the class.

Main Ideas B Answers, p. 242

Answers will vary. Sample answers:

1. Pretend play is an important activity for a child's development.
2. When children are involved in complex pretend play, they are building social and language skills.
3. When children are involved in pretend play, they learn to self-regulate.
4. Children were able to control their behavior for a longer amount of time when they were pretend playing.
5. Private speech helps children learn to self-regulate because they talk about what they are going to do and how.
6. The way children play today does not allow for many opportunities to practice self-regulation.
7. Children today can't control their behavior as well as children in the past could.
8. Pretend play is a vital activity for young children.

DETAILS (10 minutes)

1. Direct students to write details or examples to support each statement. Remind them to look back at the article to find the details and examples.
2. Have students compare answers with a partner.
3. Go over the answers with the class.

Details Answers, p. 242

Answers will vary. Sample answers:

1. For example, they learn to make compromises and take turns while they are engaged in pretend play.
2. For example, they can concentrate on one thing.
3. For example, when they are pretending to be guards at a factory, they are learning to stand still for a long period of time.
4. Video games, for example, have predetermined scripts. They tell children what to do and how to do it. Children don't have to make the rules for themselves.
5. In one experiment, children today couldn't stand still for nearly as long as children in the 1940s.

For additional practice with reading comprehension, have students visit *Q Online Practice*.

Reading and Writing 4, page 243

WHAT DO YOU THINK?

A (15 minutes)

1. Ask students to read the questions and reflect on their answers.
2. Seat students in small groups and assign roles: a group leader to make sure everyone contributes, a note-taker to record the group's ideas, a reporter to share the group's ideas with the class, and a timekeeper to watch the clock.
3. Give students five minutes to discuss the questions. Call time if conversations are winding down. Allow them an extra minute or two if necessary.
4. Then have students choose one of the questions and write a paragraph in response.
5. Call on volunteers to read their paragraphs.

What Do You Think? Activity A Answers, p. 243

Answers will vary. Sample answers:

1. If children can't self-regulate, when they get older they might not know how to get along with others.
2. The author might say that playing is learning, so children need to do it at school too.

Critical Thinking Tip (1 minute)

1. Ask a volunteer to read the tip aloud.
2. Explain: *When we hypothesize, we make an "educated guess." That means that we collect as much information on the topic as possible, analyze it, and use what we know to make a prediction. You do this in the classroom when you answer questions about the author or when you guess a word's meaning from the context.*

B (10 minutes)

1. Tell the students that they should think about both Reading 1 and Reading 2 as they discuss the questions in Activity B.
2. Call on each group's reporter to give a brief summary of their group's discussion.

What Do You Think? Activity B Answers, p. 243

Answers will vary. Sample answers:

1. I think pretend play is less important for adults. Adults should have already learned to self-regulate.
2. I think it's unhealthy for children to study so much and not have time to play. As we learned in the reading, playing is an important part of a child's emotional development.

Learning Outcome

Use the Learning Outcome to frame the purpose and relevance of Readings 1 and 2. Ask: *What did you learn from Readings 1 and 2 that prepares you to persuade readers that video games are helpful or harmful to children?* (Students learned about the importance of play and the benefits it has for both children and adults. They may want to use some of these ideas in their Unit Assignments.)

Vocabulary Skill: Collocations with prepositions (10 minutes)

1. Ask for volunteers to read the information and examples for collocations with prepositions.
2. Check comprehension: *What are some common collocation patterns? What words collocate with* rob? *What's an example of an adjective and a preposition that collocate together?*
3. List the different collocation patterns on the board and elicit additional examples.

Skill Note

Online corpora are a priceless tool in helping students to learn about a word's collocations. When students learn a new word, they can simply enter it into an online corpus, such as The Corpus of Contemporary American English (www.AmericanCorpus.org). There they will find thousands of authentic examples of how the word is used. They can see what nouns, adjectives, or verbs a preposition collocates with (or vice versa).

▶ *Reading and Writing 4, page 244*

Tip for Success (1 minute)

1. Read the tip aloud.
2. Ask students what they usually write down when they learn a new word.
3. Explain: *A learner's dictionary will often give a word's common collocations. It also will give a sample sentence. Take note of any collocations in the sample sentence.*

A (15 minutes)

1. Direct students to read the excerpts and write the correct prepositions. Suggest that they use a dictionary for help.
2. Have students compare answers with a partner.
3. Go over the answers with the class.

Vocabulary Skill A Answers, p. 244

1. about;	**2.** for;	**3.** into;	**4.** with, on;
5. to;	**6.** for;	**7.** on;	**8.** in

B (15 minutes)

1. Direct students to write five sentences with collocations and then share their sentences with a partner.
2. Ask volunteers to write their sentences on the board. Correct any errors with the collocations.

Vocabulary Skill B Answers, p. 244

Answers will vary. Sample answers:

1. I'm **concerned about** my daughter. She isn't feeling well.
2. I hope we can **incorporate** some more speaking practice **into** our Grammar class.
3. I don't think Tuan has the **ability to** relax when he's with his older brother; they're always competing with each other.
4. It's difficult to **concentrate on** the movie when someone is talking.
5. I am **working with** two co-workers **on** a new project.

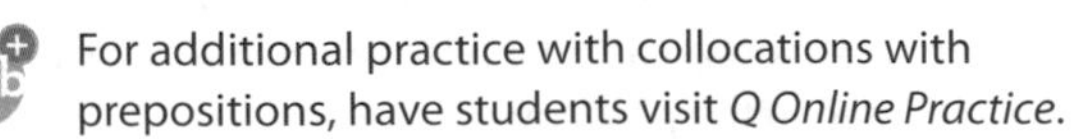

For additional practice with collocations with prepositions, have students visit *Q Online Practice*.

Reading and Writing 4, page 245

WRITING

Writing Skill: Writing a persuasive essay (10 minutes)

1. Tell students that they will write a new kind of essay: a persuasive essay. Ask students to think about a time when they wanted to convince someone that they were right.
2. Read the information together. Check comprehension: *What is the purpose of a persuasive essay? What kind of research do you need to support your position? What should your body paragraphs include?*
3. Refer students back to page 237 to review how counterarguments and refutations are presented in writing. Point out the expressions commonly used for both.

A (15 minutes)

1. Have students complete the activity individually.
2. Direct them to compare answers with a partner. Then discuss the answers as a class.

Writing Skill A Answers, pp. 245–246

Thesis: However, the truth is that competitive games are a valuable preparation for adult life.
Main idea, paragraph 2: Games with winners and losers give children the chance to experience life's ups and downs.
Main idea, paragraph 3: Children who participate in competitive games develop qualities that will allow them to succeed in the complex world of adult life.
Main idea, paragraph 4: On the negative side, there are those who will say that competition actually encourages some bad values, which does happen.

Critical Q: Expansion Activity

Identify the Author's Opinion

Give students practice with identifying the author's opinion by having them look at the thesis statement and main ideas from the essay on pages 245–246. Also, direct students to underline the counterarguments and refutations in the essay. Based on this information, have students identify the author's opinion and predict how the author would respond to the question posed in the essay's title, "Are Competitive Games Harmful to Children?"

Reading and Writing 4, page 247

Tip for Success (1 minute)

1. Ask a volunteer to read the tip aloud.
2. Have students identify the counterarguments and refutations in the essay.
3. Explain: *Including a counterargument and refutation in your writing shows that you have thought carefully about the topic. You are not just presenting your own ideas. Presenting a counterargument and refuting it makes your own argument look stronger and more credible.*

B (10 minutes)

1. Have students circle the answer to each question.
2. Elicit the answers from volunteers.

Writing Skills B Answers, p. 247

1. b; **2.** b; **3.** a; **4.** b; **5.** c; **6.** c; **7.** a

21ST CENTURY SKILLS

Employers want employees who can communicate their ideas and opinions effectively. Learning to include a concession in your writing or verbal discussions shows that you are aware of both sides of an issue. The inclusion of another point of view lends weight to your own viewpoint because you not only have to support your ideas, but you also have to express why they are better. This skill can be useful in a wide range of workplace situations, such as in persuading a customer to choose a particular product or expressing your opinion about a work policy.

web For additional practice with writing a persuasive essay, have students visit *Q Online Practice.*

Reading and Writing 4, page 248

Grammar: Adverb clauses of concession (10 minutes)

1. Ask volunteers to read the information about adverb clauses of concession.
2. Check comprehension: *What is a concession? What message does a concession send? What are some subordinators that show concession?*

Skill Note

Explain to students that using adverb clauses of concession will help them present counterarguments and refutations in their writing. Remind them that the clause that contains the adverb of concession is the counterargument that is being refuted. Using a concession clause at the beginning of a sentence puts the primary focus on that clause and draws readers' attention to the concession.

Point out that the subordinators *although* and *though* have the same meaning while *even though* is a little stronger and more emphatic. At the beginning of a sentence, *although and though* can be used interchangeably, but only *though* can be used at the end of a sentence. For example, *Recess reduces class time. It is important for children, though.*

Tip for Success (3 minutes)

1. Read the tip aloud.
2. Explain: *When the concession clause is first, you may need to use a pronoun to refer to the idea or person that you introduce later in the sentence.*
3. Point out how the pronoun *it* is used for *recess* in the two examples sentences on page 248. Provide additional examples with other pronouns, such as *he* and *she.*

A (10 minutes)

1. Direct students to combine the sentences with the subordinators in parentheses.
2. Put students in pairs to compare their answers.
3. Have volunteers put their sentences on the board and correct them together as a class.

Grammar A Answers, pp. 248–249

1. **a.** Although it is vital that they rest, children need lots of active play.
   b. While they need lots of active play, it is vital that children rest.
2. **a.** Even though it encourages bad behavior, competitive play is helpful for children.
   b. Despite the fact that it is helpful for children, competitive play encourages bad behavior.
3. **a.** While it can be a good lesson for children, losing a game is a horrible experience.
   b. While it is a horrible experience, losing a game is a good lesson for children.

Reading and Writing 4, page 249

B (10 minutes)

1. Direct students to work individually to complete each sentence with their own ideas. Then have them compare sentences with a partner.
2. Elicit sentences from volunteers. You may want students to write their sentences on the board.

Grammar B Answers, p. 249

Answers will vary. Sample answers:

1. Even though sports are difficult for some children, they can learn important skills such as teamwork and determination.
2. Although there is a lot of work to be done each day, businesses should encourage more fun activities in the office.
3. Despite the fact that not all children will take art or music, art programs should not be eliminated from schools.
4. Though people say they are too busy to relax, we should all make time to do something we enjoy each day.

For additional practice with adverb clauses of concession, have students visit *Q Online Practice*.

Reading and Writing 4, page 250

Unit Assignment: Write a persuasive essay

Unit Question (5 minutes)

Refer students back to the ideas they discussed at the beginning of the unit about the importance of play. Cue students if necessary by asking specific questions about the content of the unit: *What did we learn about the importance of play for children's development? Why is it important for adults to play as well? What are some ways in which adults' play is different from children's play?*

Learning Outcome

1. Tie the Unit Assignment to the unit Learning Outcome. Say: *The outcome for this unit is to write a persuasive essay. This Unit Assignment is going to let you show your skill in writing a persuasive essay that includes facts and evidence, counterarguments, and refutations.*
2. Explain that you are going to use a rubric similar to their Self-Assessment checklist on p. 252 to grade their unit assignment. You can also share a copy of the Unit Assignment Rubric (on p. 108 of this *Teacher's Handbook*) with the students.

Plan and Write

Brainstorm

A (15 minutes)

1. Put students into small groups to discuss the questions and complete the T-chart.

2. Suggest to students that they draw the T-chart in their notebooks, or provide each group with poster paper if they need more space.

Plan

B (20 minutes)

1. Remind students of the importance of including counterarguments and refutations. Read the instructions together. Tell students that they should fill in the chart to help them to organize their essay.
2. Students may work with a partner if they need help organizing their ideas.
3. Once students have completed their chart, they should complete the outline for their essay.

Tip for Success (1 minute)

1. Ask a volunteer to read the tip aloud.
2. Explain: *Sometimes quotations give more weight to your argument because it shows that an expert or research agrees with you. Remember to share where you found this information in order to give credit to the expert or researcher.*

▶ *Reading and Writing 4, page 252*

Write

C (20 minutes)

1. Direct students to write their essay.
2. Remind them to refer to the Self-Assessment checklist on p. 252 to guide their writing.

Alternative Unit Assignments

Assign or have students choose one of these assignments to do instead of, or in addition to, the Unit Assignment.

1. Write an essay explaining which type of play is most important for children. Use information from this unit and your own ideas. Support your opinion with reasons and examples.
2. Describe a game you enjoy or enjoyed as a child. Give a brief summary of the game and explain why you enjoy it.

For an additional Unit Assignment, have students visit *Q Online Practice*.

Revise and Edit

Peer Review

A (15 minutes)

1. Pair students and direct them to read each other's work.
2. Ask students to answer and discuss the questions.
3. Give students suggestions of helpful feedback: *This is a clear counterargument. I liked the example you gave in the third paragraph. You might want to use an adverb clause of concession in the second paragraph.*

Rewrite

B (10 minutes)

Students should review their partners' answers from A and rewrite their paragraphs if necessary.

Edit

C (10 minutes)

1. Direct students to read and complete the Self-Assessment checklist. They should be prepared to hand in their work or discuss it in class.
2. Ask for a show of hands for how many students gave all or mostly *yes* answers.
3. Use the Unit Assignment Rubric on p. 108 in this *Teacher's Handbook* to score each student's assignment.
4. Alternatively, divide the class into large groups and have students read their paragraphs to their group. Pass out copies of the Unit Assignment Rubric and have students grade each other.

▶ *Reading and Writing 4, page 253*

Track Your Success (5 minutes)

1. Have students circle the words they have learned in this unit. Suggest that students go back through the unit to review any words they have forgotten.
2. Have students check the skills they have mastered. If students need more practice to feel confident about their proficiency in a skill, point out the page numbers and encourage them to review.
3. Read the Learning Outcome aloud. Ask students if they feel that they have met the outcome.

Unit Assignment Rubric

Student name: ______________________________

Date: ____________

Unit Assignment: *Write a persuasive essay.*

20 points = Essay element was completely successful (at least 90% of the time).
15 points = Essay element was mostly successful (at least 70% of the time).
10 points = Essay element was partially successful (at least 50% of the time).
0 points = Essay element was not successful.

Write a Persuasive Essay	20 points	15 points	10 points	0 points
Essay builds a convincing argument with facts, evidence, and examples.				
Counterarguments and refutations are included.				
Adverb clauses of concession are used correctly.				
Collocations with prepositions are used correctly.				
Punctuation, spelling, and grammar are correct.				

Total points: ____________

Comments:

Welcome to the Q Testing Program

1. MINIMUM SYSTEM REQUIREMENTS[1]

1024 x 768 screen resolution displaying 32-bit color

Web browser[2]:
Windows®-requires Internet Explorer® 7 or above
Mac®-requires OS X v10.4 and Safari® 2.0 or above
Linux®-requires Mozilla® 1.7 or Firefox® 1.5.0.9 or above

To open and use the customizable tests you must have an application installed that will open and edit .doc files, such as Microsoft® Word® (97 or higher).

To view and print the Print-and-go Tests, you must have an application installed that will open and print .pdf files, such as Adobe® Acrobat® Reader (6.0 or higher).

2. RUNNING THE APPLICATION

Windows®/Mac®

- Ensure that no other applications are running.
- Insert the Q: Skills for Success Testing Program CD-ROM into your CD-ROM drive.
- Double click on the file "start.htm" to start.

Linux®

- Insert the Q: Skills for Success Testing Program CD-ROM into your CD-ROM drive.
- Mount the disk on to the desktop.
- Double click on the CD-ROM icon.
- Right click on the icon for the "start.htm" file and select to "open with Mozilla".

3. TECHNICAL SUPPORT

If you experience any problems with this CD-ROM, please check that your machine matches or exceeds the minimum system requirements in point 1 above and that you are following the steps outlined in point 2 above.

If this does not help, e-mail us with your query at: elt.cdsupport.uk@oup.com
Be sure to provide the following information:

- Operating system (e.g. Windows 2000, Service Pack 4)
- Application used to access content, and version number
- Amount of RAM
- Processor speed
- Description of error or problem
- Actions before error occurred
- Number of times the error has occurred
- Is the error repeatable?

---

[1] The Q Testing Program CD-ROM also plays its audio files in a conventional CD player.

[2] Note that when browsing the CD-ROM in your Web browser, you must have pop-up windows enabled in your Web browser settings.

The Q Testing Program

The disc on the inside back cover of this book contains both ready-made and customizable versions of **Reading and Writing** and **Listening and Speaking** tests. Each of the tests consists of multiple choice, fill-in-the-blanks/sentence completion, error correction, sentence reordering/sentence construction, and matching exercises.

Creating and Using Tests

1. Select "Reading and Writing Tests" or "Listening and Speaking Tests" from the main menu.
2. Select the appropriate unit test or cumulative test (placement, midterm, or final) from the left-hand column.
3. For ready-made tests, select a Print-and-go Test, Answer Key, and Audio Script (for Listening and Speaking tests).
4. To modify tests for your students, select a Customizable Test, Answer Key, and Audio Script (for Listening and Speaking tests). Save the file to your computer and edit the test using Microsoft Word or a compatible word processor.
5. For Listening and Speaking tests, use the audio tracks provided with the tests. **Audio files for the listening and speaking tests can also be played in a standard CD player.**

Reading and Writing Tests

Each test consists of 40 questions taken from the selected unit. The Reading and Writing Tests assess reading skills, vocabulary, vocabulary skills, grammar, and writing skills.

Listening and Speaking Tests

Each test consists of 40 questions taken from the selected unit. The Listening and Speaking Tests assess listening skills, vocabulary, vocabulary skills, grammar, pronunciation, and speaking skills.

Cumulative Tests

The placement tests for both Listening and Speaking and Reading and Writing consist of 50 questions. Each placement test places students in the correct level of *Q*: Introductory–5. **A printable User Guide to help you administer the placement test is included with the placement test files on the CD-ROM.**

The midterm tests for both Listening and Speaking and Reading and Writing consist of 25 questions covering Units 1–5 of the selected Level. The midterm Reading and Listening texts are new and not used in any other tests or student books.

The final tests for both Listening and Speaking and Reading and Writing consist of 25 questions covering Units 6–10 of the selected Level. The final Reading and Listening texts are new and not used in any other tests or student books.